THE SUSSEX OPPORTUNITY

A NEW UNIVERSITY ■AND THE FUTURE■

EDITED BY
ROGER BLIN-STOYLE
IN ASSOCIATION WITH GEOFF IVEY

THE HARVESTER PRESS

First published in Great Britain in 1986 by
THE HARVESTER PRESS LIMITED
Publisher: John Spiers, B.A. (Sussex)
16 Ship Street, Brighton, Sussex

British Library Cataloguing in Publication Data

The Sussex opportunity: a new university and the future.
1. University of Sussex – History
I. Blin-Stoyle, R.J.   II. Ivey, G.M.
378.422'56'09   LF55

ISBN 0-7108-1064-4

Typeset in Sabon 11 on 12 by Computape (Pickering) Ltd
Printed and bound in Great Britain by
Biddles Ltd, Guildford and King's Lynn

THE HARVESTER PRESS GROUP
The Harvester Group comprises Harvester Press Limited (chiefly
publishing literature, fiction, philosophy, psychology, and science
and trade books); Harvester Press Microform Publications Ltd.,
(publishing in microform previously unpublished archives, scarce
printed sources, and indexes to these collections); Wheatsheaf
Books Limited (chiefly publishing in economics, international politics, sociology, women's studies and related social sciences); Certain
Records Ltd., and John Spiers Music Ltd. (music publishing).

A publication to mark the Silver Jubilee
(1961–1986)
of the University of Sussex

Contents

Contents

List of Illustrations

The Contributors

Tony Baldry read Law in the School of Social Sciences. Called to the Bar, he practises on the Oxford Circuit and is also a director of the New Opportunity Press. He is the first former Sussex undergraduate to be elected to the House of Commons where he sits as Conservative Member for Banbury.

Fred Bayley received his first practical engineering training in workshops and at sea before graduating from King's College, Newcastle, where he later taught. He was appointed Professor of Mechanical Engineering at Sussex in 1966 and has served as Dean of the School of Engineering and Applied Sciences and as Pro-Vice-Chancellor (Science).

Roger Blin-Stoyle came to Sussex in 1962 from Oxford as Professor of Theoretical Physics and founding Science Dean. He has been Pro-Vice Chancellor, and is now on partial secondment as Chairman of the School Curriculum Development Committee. He was elected a Fellow of the Royal Society in 1976.

Victoria Bourne was born and brought up in London. While reading Russian at Sussex, she lived for a year in Moscow working for Progress Publishers. She has published several articles and is now working for the Montessori Training Organisation.

Asa Briggs, Provost of Worcester College, Oxford, was Vice-Chancellor of the University of Sussex from 1967 to 1976. Before that he was founding Dean of the School of Social Sciences and the first Pro-Vice-Chancellor. He is an historian and has written many books on nineteenth and twentieth century social and cultural history. He was made a Life Peer in 1976.

Alistair Chalmers came to Sussex in 1966 and was appointed Professor of Psychology in 1976. He was a co-founder of the Cognitive Studies Programme and has served as Dean of Social Sciences and Pro-Vice-Chancellor (Arts and Social Studies). He is now Academic Director of Computing Services.

Harry Dean read Biology at Sussex and was also Treasurer of the Students' Union. After a period working in the Science Policy Research Unit in the Armament and Disarmament Information Unit he joined London Weekend Television as a researcher and is now Producer of *Weekend World*.

Colin Eaborn was appointed as the first Professor of Chemistry in 1962 after spending 15 years at the University of Leicester. He has been Dean of the School of Molecular Sciences and Pro-Vice-Chancellor (Science). He was elected a Fellow of the Royal Society in 1970.

Michael Eraut joined the University in 1967 after doctoral research in chemistry at Cambridge and educational research at the University of Illinois. He became Reader in Education in 1976 and is Chairman-designate of the Continuing and Professional Education Area.

Chris Freeman is Phillips Professor of Science Policy at Sussex. He was educated at the London School of Economics and Sandhurst, and was formerly Director of the Science Policy Research Unit (1965 to 1981).

John Fulton was the first Vice-Chancellor of the University. Previously he was Fellow of Balliol College, Oxford (1928 to 1947) and Principal, University College of Swansea (1947 to 1959). He was Chairman of the Committee on the Civil Service (1966 to 1968) and was created a Life Peer in 1966.

Geoff Ivey worked for Reuters as a journalist in London and Madrid before joining the University's Administration. In fourteen years at Sussex he has held several posts including P.A. to the Vice-Chancellor, Secretary of Education and, currently, head of the Council Secretariat.

Michael Kenward was born and bred in Sussex. He read Physics in the (then) School of Physical Sciences and after a period of research with the UK Atomic Energy Authority went into scientific publishing. He has been Editor of the New Scientist since 1979.

Anthony Low was the founding Dean of the School of African and Asian Studies. He was subsequently Vice-Chancellor of the Australian National University (1975–82) and since 1983 has been Smuts Professor of the History of the British Commonwealth at Cambridge.

Norman MacKenzie was educated at the London School of Economics and was for twenty years assistant editor of the *New Statesman*. He came to Sussex in 1963 and among his other appointments he was Director of the School of Education and Chairman of Education. He retired in 1983 but is still busy teaching and writing and has recently completed a four-volume edition of Beatrice Webb's *Diary*, in collaboration with his wife Jeanne.

John Maynard Smith became Professor of Biology and first Dean of the School of Biological Sciences at Sussex in 1965. He is a graduate in both engineering and zoology and was previously at University College, London. He is a Fellow of the Royal Society and a Foreign Member of the National Academy of Sciences.

Margaret McGowan, who is Professor of French, has been at Sussex since 1964, having previously taught at the University of Glasgow. Her published work has included books on composite art forms, Montaigne and Renaissance poetry. She has been Dean of the School of European Studies and is currently Pro-Vice-Chancellor (Arts and Social Studies).

Nigel Savage read American Studies at Sussex, graduating in July 1985. He completed an MA in History at Georgetown University, Washington DC, and in October 1985 began working for N M Rothschild & Sons in London.

Bernard Scott came to Sussex as first Professor of Mathematics and founder of the Mathematics Subject Group from a Readership in Pure Mathematics at King's College, University of London. He was Chairman of Mathematics from 1962 to 1966 and retired in 1980.

Brian Smith is a Reader in Physics and prior to joining Sussex in 1963 taught and researched at London University and the

California Institute of Technology. He was Chairman of Community Services for six years and is currently heavily involved in the work of South East Arts.

Ken Smith came from Cambridge in 1962 as the first Professor of Experimental Physics. He has been Dean of the School of Mathematical and Physical Sciences and Chairman of the Physics Subject Group, the Discipline Committee and Counselling Services.

Denys Wilkinson is a physicist and has been Vice-Chancellor of the University since 1976. Previously he was at Cambridge University until 1957 and then at Oxford University as Head of the Department of Nuclear Physics. He is a Fellow of the Royal Society and was knighted in 1974.

Donald Winch is Professor of the History of Economics and has been at Sussex since 1962, having served as Dean of the School of Social Sciences from 1968 to 1974. He was educated at the London School of Economics and Princeton University and has published work on the history of social and political theory as well as economic thought and policy.

Foreword

Roger Blin-Stoyle

In the summer of 1961, whilst Fellow of an Oxford college, I learned that a university was about to come into being in one of my favourite counties – Sussex. Stimulated by a sabbatical year just spent at the Massachusetts Institute of Technology, unhappy about the then structure of Oxford physics degree courses and frustrated by the sluggishness of the wheels of change in Oxford, I applied for the post of Professor of Theoretical Physics in this first of the 'new' universities. As a consequence I found myself in October 1962 as Dean of its first science School, the School of Physical Sciences. Since then, from a variety of positions, through to and including that of Acting Vice-Chancellor, I have observed and experienced its development over 25 exciting years. Most recently, partially seconded from the University to chair the School Curriculum Development Committee, my prime emotional and intellectual commitment has lain elsewhere and I have been able to reflect on the University's development much more objectively than in the past. How, in a few words, do I see this development?

Certainly I and, I believe, all of those who came in the very early years have never regretted the gamble we took in leaving the secure confines of Oxbridge or elsewhere to tackle the uncertain and ambitious (audacious?) task of setting up a new university from scratch. We were fortunately unencumbered, as developing university colleges had been in the past, by the need to tailor our thinking to the external degree requirements of London University. Subject to the general approval of the Academic Advisory Committee we were completely free to structure courses as we pleased and this was a unique and challenging opportunity which was grasped enthusiastically.

Things moved very quickly and in the first two or three years the style and ethos of the University were firmly established.

The work and ideas of these early years were described fully in *The Idea of a New University* (ed. David Daiches) published in 1964, which is referred to frequently in this book. Suffice it to say here that much of our thinking was characterised by the conviction that our undergraduate courses and academic organisation should provide for the full exploitation of interdisciplinary studies. Hence the formation of Schools of Studies* rather than Departments, and the commitment to 'Contextual' studies on the Arts and Social Studies side of the University and to the 'Major/Minor' degree structure on the Science side. Much as all of us have yearned (some, very strongly) from time to time for the cosiness, tidiness and relative simplicity of a departmental structure and in spite of the rather complex organisation necessary to sustain the School of Studies system, it has stood the test of time. The stimulation and illumination of working closely with other disciplines having different intellectual traditions, work styles and viewpoints has amply compensated for the periodical organisational frustrations.

The content and structure of our degree courses and the ways in which they are assessed have, of course, changed over the years and much of this is described in the essays in this volume dealing with academic matters, but by and large the courses still retain the style originally established. In particular, interdisciplinarity features in many of them and in a coherent way – we have totally eschewed the *à la carte* approach to their formulation.

Research has undoubtedly prospered; indeed, as will be clear from some of the essays, it is of high distinction. Those of us

---

* There are now five undergraduate Schools of Studies in the Arts and Social Studies Area: African and Asian Studies (AFRAS), Cultural and Community Studies (CCS), English and American Studies (ENGAM), European Studies (EURO) and Social Sciences (SOCS). In the Science Area there are four Schools of Studies: Biological Sciences (BIOLS), Chemistry and Molecular Sciences (MOLS), Engineering and Applied Sciences (EAPS) and Mathematical and Physical Sciences (MAPS). There are no Schools of Studies in the Education Area, virtually all of whose students are postgraduates. The organisation of the University's academic work in the large is through the three Areas just mentioned and there are no

responsible for bringing the University into being were always absolutely clear (unlike some in high places today) that a high level of research and scholarly activity was vital, not only because research and scholarship contribute so much to the general ethos of a university, but also because, without them, teaching at university level can become lifeless, uninspired and dated. Much of this research is typical of that in many universities but there is some that strongly reflects the Sussex interdisciplinary thrust and this is exemplified particularly in the two essays on Cognitive Studies and on the Science Policy Research Unit.

In undertaking the tasks of teaching, scholarship and research the academic staff have been supported by an administration which has done its job well. Initially it was inevitably highly centralised; then, as we expanded, a devolved pattern was adopted in which it was felt that the administrators in the Arts and Social Studies, Science and Education Areas were primarily 'loyal' to the academics in those Areas – they were on their sides. But the financial exigencies of the last few years have led to a recentralisation (shades of Jarratt?) and a loss of 'local' administrators. There are now tensions not present before. But tensions are part and parcel of evolution and will no doubt reduce to insignificance as, with the university system as a whole, we fight to preserve our integrity.

What of the tens of thousands of undergraduate and graduate students who have passed through the University since its foundation? The views and reactions of a few of them are included in this volume, but it is clearly impossible to generalise. We have tried to provide stimulating courses and research opportunities and to encourage our students to think, reflect (the University motto is 'Be Still and Know') and question. We leave it to those who have interacted with them since they have left Sussex to judge how effective we have been.

Of course, instant judgements about our students and, for that matter, about the University, have been made by the local community. The University has made a considerable impact

---

conventional faculties; but the reader should note that the word 'faculty' is generally used to connote members of the academic staff.

on Brighton and Sussex and one of the essays explores the evolution and nature of our relationship with this community. It has been a variable one but one which has generated many firm formal and informal bonds as well as friendships. Certainly, the University is now regarded with pride, if sometimes cautiously, and as being an important part of the Brighton 'scene'.

The University has had three Vice-Chancellors during its first twenty-five years – John Fulton (Lord Fulton*) who fathered the University into being and to whom I and many others owe so much for his vision, kindness and gentle, but *so* effective, guidance during the formative years; Asa Briggs (Lord Briggs) who from the outset injected many of the creative and exciting ideas which have characterised this University; and Denys Wilkinson (Sir Denys Wilkinson) who has presided over the University during its most difficult period fighting to preserve all that is excellent in its teaching and research. They each present their views on the development of the University with John Fulton in his 'Afterword' reflecting on the extent to which early expectations have been fulfilled. Together with the other essays the hope is that this volume gives a realistic account, warts and all, of the way in which the first of the new universities has not only come of age but has reached maturity and is ready to move forward into the future.

In conclusion, I would like to thank all those who have made this book possible: the contributors who have given freely of their time and responded to my request for essays with exemplary promptitude; the Harvester Press which has given generous help in publishing the book and has agreed that profits should benefit the University's association for former students – the University of Sussex Society; and my Associate Editor, Geoff Ivey, who, with tact and firmness, has tried to ensure that the editing process was carried out carefully and responsibly.

––––––

Sadly, as this book was going to press, I learned of John Fulton's death – on Friday 14 March 1986. This book can, therefore, perhaps be regarded as a partial memorial to the educational endeavours of this much loved and highly respected man.

1

The Years of Plenty, 1961–1976

Asa Briggs

Those of us who were living and working in the University of Sussex between 1961 and 1976 were not conscious of the fact that we were experiencing years of plenty, least of all during the very early years. What we were conscious of, however, particularly during those early years in the University's life, was that we were living through an exciting period of unprecedented opportunity. It was unavoidable – and healthy – that we did not usually find it easy to consider what we were doing in historical perspective. There was too much to do. I believe that I was alone in collecting the ephemera of the earliest days on the grounds that they would one day be of historical interest, but as the University grew there was little time even for me to do this. Only seldom did I have time to keep a diary. Outsiders wrote more about the University of Sussex, some of it flattering, some of it nonsense, than we did ourselves.

The term 'plenty' is meaningful only if the 1960s, to which we undoubtedly belonged as a new creation, are contrasted with the 1980s, a bleak decade in British university history. Sussex had its origins, however, in the late 1950s. We were very much a pre-Robbins university. I was a member of the University Grants Committee (and of its New Universities Sub-Committee) during the late 1950s and took an active part in crucial pre-Robbins debates about the implications of what were called, sometimes a little pompously, 'Bulge' and 'Trend', the demographic and social forces which, through statistics of the size of school sixth forms, pointed to the need for an increased university population. If the existing universities had responded to the need, there would have been fewer new universities, a solution which later on many of them

1

favoured. As it was, the existing universities failed completely to respond to the challenge – this was not their golden age – and the University Grants Committee had to act. It owed much to its Chairman and to the imagination and drive of a number of its members, and it did not need Robbins to prompt it.

The new universities before and after Robbins never worked as a bloc, although many outsiders believed that they did. Nor did they follow one pattern. This I consider was wise. The tendency to apply formulae to universities during the 1970s and 1980s carries with it many dangers. There were general financial worries about university expansion inside the University Grants Committee on the eve of the Robbins Report, however, and it is significant that in 1962, in the second year of the University of Sussex, an uninspired Treasury pruned and pared the university grant suggested by the University Grants Committee. This was apparently the first time that such a thing had happened. It was not a good omen. The Robbins Report, accepted with extraordinary speed by the government and (to the horror of myself and some other members) never discussed as such by the University Grants Committee, by then under a far less effective new Chairman, was responsible for the government providing more funds. A large share of them went to universities which had failed to show any initiative during the 1950s. The physical effects of the so-called 'affluence' of the period are more visible still in the older than the new universities. Indeed, at the time the new universities were given very carefully rationed funds which were more closely scrutinised than those of older universities. My own private papers reveal the financial difficulties we often faced. Fortunately, the Finance Officer of the University was extremely able in judging what we could and could not do.

Like other new universities we had an Academic Advisory Committee to guide us through our first years. It included some distinguished members, some of whom, particularly its Chairman, Sir James Duff, were keenly interested in our progress. Yet while it generated ideas, it sensibly did not seek to go far in shaping the new university. It left planning to the first academics who, despite differences of background, experience and temperament, constituted a formidable team who could sort out complex issues, reach decisions quickly and then speak out clearly with (more or less) one common voice. Very soon, indeed, the Academic Advisory Committee was dissolved. Those of us now called 'founding fathers', although we never used the term, all felt that Brighton was a good place for the first of Britain's new universities and that, if anything, the timing of its creation had been too long delayed. We all wanted, too, to create a university which would be different. This was not because we were attracted to novelty for novelty's sake (this was anathema to me personally) or because we were preoccupied with image-building (a fashionable term at the time for reasons which had nothing to do with education). We were dissatisfied with aspects of the existing university pattern and keen to innovate. We believed that innovation was necessary in the interests of society, not ignoring the economy, and of culture, which many people now ignore. We were strongly motivated people, yet I consider we got the balance right. We felt a sense of privilege in being allowed to build a new university. Our morale was high, and we were sometimes accused outside Sussex of being 'superior' and of inflating our ambition. It would be fairer to say that we refused to think of Sussex as an 'inferior' institution, not least in relation to Oxford and Cambridge. We were completely free from the status inhibitions of some of our colleagues in other provincial universities. We did not use the term 'morale': we spoke of élan.

The crucial discussions about the shape of the University were 'internal' discussions, and the first, and most crucial of them, were held in the house of John Fulton, the first Vice-Chancellor, then called the Principal, in 1960 and 1961 before the first 52 students were admitted, and before any of the handful of academic faculty of the University who were then involved in them were working at Sussex or were on its pay roll. It was then that decisions were taken on the organisation of the University in 'Schools of Studies' rather than in Departments; on the range of the first groups of Schools; on the procedures for choosing students; on modes of teaching (principally tutorials), with a strong emphasis on students' being encouraged to learn for themselves; on the curriculum; and on the sequence of work to be followed by students, beginning with common Preliminary papers to be studied by all Sussex undergraduates. The thinking behind this process was summarised in the 1964 study, edited by David Daiches, *The Idea of a New University*. Most of the thinking remains relevant in the 1980s in completely changed circumstances, although in the short run there is now a greater demand for very specific single-subject degrees. Some of the thinking the University of Sussex has cast on one side itself in its later phases, not necessarily to its advantage.

The idea of this particular new university – and it was very carefully and critically thought out – undoubtedly appealed in 1961 and later to large numbers of sixth-formers, with girls particularly prominent in the first and early intakes. The experience of the first year when the 52 pioneering students (chosen by the Vice-Chancellor and the Registrar on the basis of the least detailed of all prospectuses) studied and worked together in two Victorian houses in Brighton remains unforgettable. It was like living in a kibbutz. At a party at the beginning of the second year, when we had moved to the new, largely undeveloped site at Falmer, one first-year girl student said to me rightly that it would never be the same again. Thereafter the experience of every year in the first decade was unique partly because numbers of students and faculty varied immensely; partly because new subjects and Schools were introduced, thereby changing the mix; partly because the physical appearance of the new campus was radically different in different years; partly because the chemistry of the mix – some would call it the sociology – was different; partly because different broad issues were raised outside the University at different times, like relations with the Polytechnic, with the College of Education and, not least, with the local community.

Yet while no two years were like each other, we – not least the students – were deeply concerned about the long run. In the beginning the students, who knew far more about the University and how it worked than students in any other university, had to do without amenities (including sports facilities) that students in other universities could enjoy. There was certainly no plenty for them: nor was there for academic faculty teaching in terrapins. Neither was the University Grants Committee ever able to help us adequately with halls of residence (we all disliked the term) – at first on grounds of principle – and we had to turn to outside sources of finance, difficult to mobilise, in order to develop the campus (one of several American terms we adopted). In what we all thought of as 'laying foundations' (in physical planning, of course, we were not always completely successful) we had to be perpetually resourceful. From the start we were forced also to attach central importance to the planning process and how best to carry it out. Before I became Vice-Chancellor in 1967 I had been for three years Pro-Vice-Chancellor Planning. It was not an empty title. I knew every member of faculty so that the planning took account of people as well as of numbers.

The key papers for the early years, when our formal constitution resembled that of most other universities and our procedures diverged, were the reports of the Buildings Committee – the first of them was held at Marlborough House on the Old Steine in Brighton in December 1961 – and the documents headed 'Logistics of Development'. The Buildings Committee meetings, chaired in the first years by Lord Shawcross, later to become second Chancellor of the University, were often dramatic: indeed, they were bound to be with Sir Basil Spence as architect. There was less drama in the academic build-up, but just as much planning. The first of the 'Logistics of Development' papers was dated 22 October 1962, and before the third of them had been accepted it was clear that undergraduate/faculty figures would rise sharply as a result of the government's acceptance of the Robbins Report. The first Vice-Chancellor had conceived of a university with 3000 students. This was not unrealistic, although some of his fellow Vice-Chancellors thought, perhaps with Keele in mind, that he was inordinately ambitious. The detailed Logistics of Development paper of 23 September 1964 shows how realistic we were at that stage: 'It has become abundantly clear', a paragraph in it read, 'that there would be disadvantages in seeking to expand the University above 3000 in 1967/68 and that the rate of growth will slacken very considerably after 1967/68.'

The Logistics of Development papers were prepared by

myself and Roger Blin-Stoyle, who was appointed as Professor of Physics and Dean of the School of Physical Sciences
in 1962. He succeeded me as second Pro-Vice-Chancellor
when I became Pro-Vice-Chancellor Planning. I do not believe
that any university development exercise was undertaken
more systematically. We took into account the total number
of undergraduates in arts, social studies and science (in some
subjects demand was running at more than 20 applicants per
place) and the total number of postgraduate students (from
the start we attracted many such students, far more than the
Academic Advisory Committee had contemplated, including
many from overseas) before calculating the total number of
faculty required in each subject: 'The more that we rely on a
"table of growth",' we stated, 'the easier it will be to plan
appointments for one, two or three years ahead, and this
offers great flexibility. Such a table should, as far as possible,
be worked out according to agreed criteria rather than on the
basis of subject bargaining power.'

Arts, social studies (I preferred this term to social sciences in
the School of which I was first Dean) and sciences were kept in
balance at Sussex before and after I became Vice-Chancellor.
Our ways of working diverged, but planning procedures were
common to all. The initial 'agreed criteria' included for arts,
where more guidance was given than in the sciences, a
standard teaching load of 12 hours of tutorials for each
member of faculty, including professors, who were given no
special privileges at Sussex in this respect, with lectures
excluded from the calculations. (The first faculty included
some brilliant lecturers who actually liked to lecture and
needed no Logistics of Development papers to lure them to the
rostrum.) An equally important criterion was a minimum
complement of four members of faculty for each subject. We
did not seek to introduce new subjects – and there was often
great pressure to do this – if they were to be understaffed. Also
rightly deemed important was 'the exclusion from the University curriculum of subjects where a large number of staff would
be required to teach a small number of students', unless such
subjects played an 'important part in the overall academic
strategy of a School'. Given the Sussex arts and social studies
curriculum there had to be agreement also about 'the need for

teachers from different subjects to teach common papers', and 'the desirability of cross-subject teaching'. (Some members of faculty were extraordinarily versatile). Finally, it was stated firmly in the September 1964 paper that 'agreement is necessary well in advance to the start of new Schools or to the introduction of new subjects'.

The planning procedures laid down in these papers were in advance of the then relatively unsophisticated planning procedures of the University Grants Committee of which I remained a member until I became Vice-Chancellor. Indeed, I was active as a member of that Committee in pressing, along with lively officers like Richard Griffiths, for a change in the way in which that body planned its increasingly complex and costly estimates. Procedures, of course, are instrumental. The objectives have to be clearly stated. In Sussex, where we stated them very explicitly, we had to stay firmly within the frame of limited public funds, and even before their vulnerability became fully apparent we wanted to get the best value for money. We were greatly helped by lay members of our Council, notably by its Chairman, Sydney Caffyn. They had as strong a sense of public accountability as any government auditor, but they had imagination too when they helped us to relate resources to objectives. A note of realism ran through all our financial papers between 1961 and 1966. Thus, we declared firmly in September 1964 that 'we must not overstrain finances this quinquennium'.

The visit of the University Grants Committee on 18 January 1966 was a happy and successful one. We were in step at that time. The last visit which I hosted in November 1975 was less so, largely because the Chairman and some members of the Committee had not fully acquainted themselves with the distinctive pattern of Sussex before they came and could not ask the knowledgeable and, when necessary, searching questions. We were disappointed with their approach, for they were less willing to learn from such university visits than members of the Committee had been during the 1950s.

The whole system of regular visits, usually called in overdignified language visitations, was to break down, of course, under the pressure first of inflation, then of cuts. Whatever my or my colleagues' views at Sussex of the fairness of University

Grants Committee quinquennial awards – and the issue was to become an important one in the 1980s – we could not have planned and created a new university if there had not been a national planning process. And at its best, when the University Grants Committee had less work to do than in the late 1960s and had not devolved an important part of its functions to subject Committees of necessarily varying degrees of knowledge and ability, the quinquennial system provided a good framework for university development. It also allowed for a proper exchange of views.

We told the University Grants Committee in 1966 in a general paper which I wrote on the University that 'the decision to establish seven new universities in the 1960s ... was regarded by all those concerned in the early stages of planning the University of Sussex as a challenge to experiment both boldly and wisely.' By then there were nine Schools, each with a Dean. I was very anxious, having reacted sharply against the departmental system, that they should not become super-departments; in other words, that we should not be exchanging sovereign states for empires, and for this reason insisted on the importance of students being able to study the same Major subject in different Schools within different Contextual frames and of academic faculty being allowed to belong to more than one School. There was far greater flexibility within the Sussex Schools system both for students and for academic faculty than there was in the Schools system of some of the other new universities. It was difficult, however, to work out an entirely satisfactory organisational pattern, and, as the University grew, even by 1966, some new members of faculty, despite more 'initiation' into Sussex than in most universities, did not really understand the system. Nor were some of them, particularly specialists concerned with their standing in their own subject, necessarily in sympathy with it. Finally the different Schools did not succeed equally well in establishing themselves as social as well as academic units. The warmth of the departmental system at its best was sometimes missing. So, too, was the intimacy of the college system which was deliberately rejected as a possibility at Sussex in 1960. I knew too much about the atmosphere of Oxford and Cambridge colleges (and of how they were financed) to feel that we could imitate them at Sussex or produce attractive alternative versions of our own. I was forced to recognise, however, by the time I became Vice-Chancellor, that people could get lost at Sussex if the Deans of Schools and a high proportion of members of faculty ignored their social responsibilities.

The first four Schools were Social Studies, European Studies (a pioneering School which having begun as an idea of Brighton's Director of Education, Bill Stone, a member of the Academic Advisory Committee, on the simple grounds that Brighton was geographically near to the Continent, soon acquired a distinctive identity under the Deanship of Martin Wight), English (and American) Studies, and Physical Sciences, with Roger Blin-Stoyle as Dean. The School of African and Asian Studies followed in October 1964: it was based on an idea of my own, and I was fortunate enough to be able to attract Anthony Low as first Dean. I had met him in Australia in 1960 when I was considering at a proper distance and in relative quiet what the Sussex 'map of learning' – my favourite metaphor – would be. I gave what to me was a significant lecture there with this title, and I was deeply impressed by Low's knowledge both of Africa and of Asia.

Educational Studies followed in 1964, and Molecular Sciences, Biological Sciences, and Applied Sciences in 1965. The relatively late arrival of these three Science Schools was due to the need to build laboratories. Yet there had been important discussions about biological sciences long before the School was started, and the views of the Royal Society on the need to develop interdisciplinary work in the life sciences had strongly influenced my own attitudes towards interdisciplinarity and the desirability of a School rather than a departmental organisation. One distinguished professor who did not come to the University but went instead to the United States, Jim Danielli, played as important a part in these discussions as any of the 'founding fathers' themselves.

I had to fight hard personally for a School of Applied Sciences, but was fortunate to be backed by one member of the University Grants Committee with whom I always worked closely, Willis Jackson. We owed much to such informed help from outside. It was a difficult fight, however, for there were

9

people in the University Grants Committee, including its then Chairman, who were uneasy about this particular Sussex bid, and I could raise no financial and little moral support from engineering firms in Sussex whose aid I invoked. Industry was not ready, although there was to be creative cooperation with industry further afield during my Vice-Chancellorship.

To me a new university was incomplete unless it had at least one School with a technological base. I was clear in the 1960s about the importance of new technology to the British economy and society and of the importance of electronics, communications technology and materials science. I found, unfortunately, that Toby Weaver, a clever and powerful but dangerous influence in the Department of Education and Science, refused dogmatically to believe that an academic like myself, or a university like ours, could or should move in the direction in which I wanted us to move; and I failed to persuade either him or Anthony Crosland, who was much under his influence, that Sussex was the right place to merge or to integrate Polytechnic and University which were geographically close to each other. Department of Education and Science 'solutions' to the problems of the 1980s, which are canvassed as if they are completely new, were very much in our minds in Sussex in the mid-1960s and were turned down then by the DES. We were to suffer a further blow when the College of Education, which quite deliberately had been sited across the road from the University in order to share in its life, passed by DES decision to the Polytechnic. The memory of the bureaucratic rigidity of at least one key official in the DES on this and similar decisions in other parts of the country – for example, on the issue of the future of Bishop Otter College in Chichester, linked to the University of Sussex – still shocks me. At least Toby Weaver had intelligence.

I have bracketed official attitudes to technology and to education together because in both these cases the Department of Education and Science came into the picture as well as the University Grants Committee, and in a period of expansion it was not a Department which inspired great confidence before or after higher education became one of its responsibilities in the aftermath of the Robbins Report. At the top level of Secretary of State, David Eccles and Edward Boyle were conspicuously far ahead of their officers in vision and in energy. The former was present at the first official dinner of the University of Sussex, when we could all assemble – students, faculty and Council – in Brighton Pavilion, and the latter was a deeply respected Pro-Chancellor of the University of Sussex before he moved to Leeds as Vice-Chancellor.

Both Eccles and Boyle had the wisdom to see that the country needed centres of higher education which would be centres of ideas as well as centres of service, and Boyle was particularly interested in the extension of our School of Educational Studies to become a School of Cultural and Community Studies under the same Dean, Boris Ford, in 1971. It is a convenient fallacy for some recent writers on higher education to claim with hindsight that the makers of the new universities in the 1960s were insensitive to some of the central issues in educational policy which dominate the 1980s. It was the opposition to the idea of Applied Sciences at Sussex, and the apathy on the part of local people who should have been interested, which stands out most in my mind in retrospect, along with the superficial way of dealing with the problems of teacher education and the development of the Polytechnic. Fortunately, the School of Applied Sciences was able to acquire as first Dean, John West, with a very broad approach to the curriculum and with an insider's knowledge of its economic and social implications. Like Anthony Low and several other active personalities in the Sussex of the 1960s, he was to move on to a Vice-Chancellorship.

Education was fortunate also in many of the people associated with it. Manny Eppel, strongly backed by me as Vice-Chancellor, developed a different approach to extramural education, concentrating on continuing education in a community setting; and Norman MacKenzie and others devised a new approach also to what came to be called educational technology, a better term than the outmoded but then still current audiovisual aids. There were many problems, but Sussex became a designated national centre, and the work carried out in the University on a battery of learning methods influenced many other institutions, including the Open University. There were some members of the faculty who were either uninterested in or critical of these developments, but

11

they appealed to members of Council like Leslie Farrer-Brown and Donald Tyerman, and they left their mark.

It is impossible to write university history without referring specifically to personalities, although some historians have tried to do so. The School of Molecular Sciences with Colin Eaborn as Dean was extremely fortunate to be able to attract chemistry faculty of the highest calibre, including one Nobel Prize winner, and by the time I left Sussex I was extremely proud of it. The library, which was one of Spence's best buildings, owed much to its first librarian, Denis Cox, who was appointed before any member of the academic faculty, including myself. The beautiful Meeting House had Daniel Jenkins as its first chaplain. The work of the School of African and Asian Studies was put into a completely different context when, largely as a result of the personal influence of Sir Andrew Cohen, the national Institute of Development Studies was located not in Oxford, but in Sussex.

The reasoning behind the decision which, like John Fulton, I pressed for and believe to have been the right one, raises different questions, however, from those of personality, just as the development of technology and of education did. A 'centre of excellence' argument was deliberately rejected at the national level in favour of the argument that an institute concerned largely with what was coming to be called the Third World might be less cramped in a new university committed to African and Asian Studies than in an old university where there was a greater concentration of professional expertise but where African and Asian Studies tended to be peripheral. The decision in 1965 to site the Institute at Sussex was psychologically of the utmost importance and it had wide-ranging implications.

One of them was the sense of the University of Sussex as a research university (with the research, when possible, linked to teaching), where institutes and centres, financed in different ways but only to a limited extent, if at all, by the University Grants Committee, would concern themselves with major national and international themes, again where appropriate, in an interdisciplinary way. A Centre for Contemporary European Studies was one of them: it was created at the appropriate time and established close links with a wide range of outside bodies and with European institutions in Brussels and elsewhere. (Its first Director was to join the staff of the Commission in Brussels, as was one of my personal assistants as Vice-Chancellor.)

I took a personal interest in many of the institutes and centres, some of which, like the Agricultural and Food Research Council-sponsored Unit of Nitrogen Fixation and the Astronomy Centre, which hosted the most impressive international gathering of my Vice-Chancellorship, the 14th General Assembly of the Astronomical Union in 1970, were in the field of science. I appreciated, however, that they might have difficulties in acquiring or maintaining adequate core finance to sustain a programme deriving variable income from projects and that there would inevitably be a high mortality rate. I do not regret the policy. It put Sussex on a different map from the map of learning. For a time through the Centre for Multi-Racial Studies we were even able to have valuable academic links with the West Indies.

We were careful to use the simple term 'Centre' rather than the more grand title of 'Institute' when there were possible financial or other hazards, and we sometimes used the term 'Unit' as well. The Unit which I conceived and which was closest to my own heart was the Science Policy Research Unit which was fortunate to attract men of the calibre and character of Christopher Freeman, its first Director, and of Geoffrey Oldham, its second. At that time there was no other unit of this kind in any other university. It has a fascinating history of its own, fascinating enough even in its early phases to attract the beneficence of Reginald M. Phillips, the University's biggest single private benefactor. I had almost weekly tutorials with Phillips throughout my Vice-Chancellorship, some of the most gruelling but fruitful tutorials in my academic experience. He was personally more interested in philately than in science policy – he had presented his famous collection to the nation to found the National Postal Museum – and he also endowed a Philatelic Unit at the University which doubtless raised some academic eyebrows. It brought the University into direct contact, however, with the Post Office and its leading officials, with interesting by-products – just as the Science Policy Research Unit brought it into extremely close contact with the Department of Trade and Industry. There was sometimes a clearer recognition there of how universities can best function in the late twentieth century than there was in the Department of Education and Science.

SPRU, as it was soon called, was associated in my own mind not only with external contacts but with the so-called Arts/ Science Scheme inside the University. Much thought went into its structure and content, and although it changed its pattern sometimes in an evolutionary, often in a jerky, fashion, its objectives were plain – to give all arts and social science students in the University some understanding either of a science or of science policy and all students of science some acquaintance with the humanities or with the procedures of the social sciences. The success of the scheme depended on a willing involvement on the part of faculty of the University, and Michael Brown was very closely associated with me in seeking to secure the necessary level of involvement. Like similar innovating schemes in the early years, Sussex owed nothing to student pressure, and it was not always easy to engage students in its work. Academic innovation during the 1960s was faculty-led, not student-led, despite a burst of student rhetoric in most universities during the last years of the decade.

In this brief and necessarily selective account of development during the first years of Sussex I have covered changes before and after I became Vice-Chancellor. There was no sharp break at that time since John Fulton and I had worked extremely closely together and most of the developments which I have noted earlier either followed consequentially on each other or were the result of initiatives which might have been taken before or after 1967. There were changes in student attitudes and activities, however, after 1967, which demand a study in themselves. They were often ill-conceived and diverted attention away from the effective work of the University, and although they involved less disruption than there was in most of the other new universities and some of the old ones, they received a disproportionate share of attention and often provoked hasty and prejudiced reactions on the part of people outside the University. What was happening at

Sussex was part of far bigger international political and cultural patterns, and it was essential for the Vice-Chancellor to try to understand it while maintaining the daily flow of university business.

The most important changes at the beginning of my Vice-Chancellorship in 1967 were organisational and can be explained in terms of the growth of the University as an institution. They were clearly set out in the ninth *Annual Report* of the University, and my views on the reorganisation and on later developments during my Vice-Chancellorship are best traced in the *Annual Reports* which I presented to the University Court. 'It was during the year 1967/68', I wrote, 'that our newness came to matter less than our size.' By then there were over 3000 students and 197 members of faculty (including research staff) and rates of growth had slackened. There was necessary realism, too, about financial resources. In the words of my address to the Court, the University Grants Committee offered the University 'considerably less than we had hoped, and in the light of our budget we had to make substantial changes to the academic plans which we had drawn up, we believed, not unrealistically.' 'There will be relatively little scope from University Grants Committee funds', I went on, 'for any large-scale new developments between now and 1972. Two consequences follow from this – first, we have to make the very best use of our resources to get full value for money, particularly in a period of continuing rising prices; second, if we wish to develop – and there is always a far greater desire in this particular University to develop than there is to consolidate – we have to attract development funds from other sources.' The messages of the 1980s were not unknown to the 1960s.

The important constitutional changes which were made in 1967 followed the preparation in the last months of John Fulton's Vice-Chancellorship of an independent report we had called for from McKinsey and Company into the government, organisation and administrative methods of the University. It was the first of its kind in a British university. The report was fully discussed and its recommendations in many respects modified as a result of the discussion. The main changes were agreed upon with little dissent – a streamlining

15

of committees, an increase in participation, a clearer definition of administrative responsibilities, greater devolution, a strengthening of the planning process and an improved system of internal communication.

The large number of specialist committees was drastically reduced, and a number of the most important of them, familiar in all British civic universities, disappeared completely, like the Academic Board and the Finance and General Purposes Committee of Council. Business was now to be channelled through four main committees – Arts and Social Studies, Science, Social Policy and Planning – before reaching Senate and Council. The work of each of the first three committees was to be the special concern of a particular university officer. The Planning Committee, which included lay members of the Council and its Chairman, was *the* key committee. It had no exact parallel in any other British university, and the quality of life in the University depended on its knowledge and drive as well as on its management of resources. The Senate, always a large and sometimes an unwieldy body, acquired student members through the device of a Senate Committee which saved the University from changes of Charter. As a result of devolution, however, much of its business had been settled before its meetings began. This was true of Council meetings also, although it was important that they should not be thought of merely as rubber-stamping. There were too many able people on Council to make that possible, and as questions of industrial relations loomed larger in the late 1960s and early 1970s the experience in this field of some members of Council was invaluable.

As a result of the changes Barry Supple, my successor as Dean of the School of Social Studies, became Chairman of Arts and Social Studies and Colin Eaborn Chairman of Science. They worked very closely with me, as did their successors. Geoffrey Lockwood became Planning Officer, and for a short time I had a small Vice-Chancellor's Office team to assist me. Brian Smith became involved with social policy and did much to deal with some of the most complex issues of the late 1960s and early 1970s relating to student accommodation, community relations on the campus (we were very much a community ourselves) and with relations with

Brighton – very much a distinctive community in its own right and one which I got to know very well.

Academic development after 1967 is summarised in some of the most important essays in this book which deal in detail with the different subject areas. The effect of devolution in 1967 was to transfer most of the discussions about particular subjects, old or new, or about interdisciplinary courses away from the centre and it gave me more time to deal with administration.

I became keenly interested in the management of universities, fully aware that the efficient working of what was coming to be called for the first time 'a university system' would become an increasingly important preoccupation in the future. I never believed that there was one single set of answers: the system for me had to allow for diversity. I believed also that management could not be separated from academic planning or from university politics. I had to be particularly sensitive to the latter at Sussex for there were many people of ability and drive in the University who had strong and incompatible views about what mattered most and about how to deal with people who disagreed with them. They never cancelled each other out. Considerable political skills were employed inside the University which would have been more usefully employed outside.

They raised some interesting academic questions, of course. It had been part of the constitutional changes of 1967 that Subject Groups were given formal recognition as well as Schools, and while I did not regard this change as in any way subversive of the Schools system, it clearly influenced discussion on interdisciplinary courses, having a tendency in practice to multiply them rather than to strengthen them. It also strengthened the position of second-generation academics in the University who had been appointed as subject specialists. Some interdisciplinary or shared courses had already proved far more successful than others. *The Modern European Mind*, for example, was far more successful than *Contemporary Britain*. When Deans began to be elected rather than appointed, there was a danger that 'vision' might be lost. There was also a danger that Arts – never a very satisfactory term – and Science might diverge.

If there was any student pressure at this time, it was for more of an *à la carte* curriculum, which I never favoured, and for changes in the examination system, which on the whole I did. There was also far more ideological talk about the curriculum: this was a feature of the late 1960s and early 1970s, and it alienated some of my colleagues. In such circumstances it was a great help to me as Vice-Chancellor that I continued to do some history teaching and met undergraduates in a different context from the Students' Union, the officers of which I met regularly, and some of whom became and remain friends.

Within the small working group of Pro-Vice-Chancellors Arts and Science and through Social Policy I was particularly anxious to establish my own priorities to try to ensure that the School of Biological Sciences, which I regarded as strategically important, was given every encouragement; that work in psychology, which had developed in different Schools and in different guises under powerful influences like those of Stuart Sutherland and Marie Jahoda, should, if possible, be brought closer together and, as an area of strength, be further strengthened; that music should be introduced into the curriculum (the visual arts already had been) even though it was not easy to introduce new subjects at this relatively late stage in the University's early history; and that, if possible, there should be one new science-based School possibly in environmental studies or in communications studies. In trying to achieve these priorities the main obstacles were entrenched interests – it is remarkable how quickly these congeal in a university – not alternative ideas.

We were not able to create a further new School nor to raise outside funds for a Centre of Communications Studies which, in my view, would have been as attractive in the long run as the Science Policy Research Unit. It was possible, however, with fairly general support, to develop operational research and through Patrick Rivett to establish links with Lancaster University, and entirely on our own and without central planning to move into linguistic and cognitive sciences, this time drawing on additional resources from Edinburgh University. My last academic act as Vice-Chancellor was to chair the Committee which brought John Lyons to Sussex as Professor of Linguistics.

There was one other ambition which took up a great deal of my time and that of my last Pro-Vice-Chancellor, Michael Thompson (my own choice, with whom I worked very closely indeed and very happily), that of developing medical education at Sussex. We failed there for reasons which had nothing to do with our planning, but we won the enthusiastic support of the local medical profession and of senior professors of medicine outside Sussex.

Throughout my Vice-Chancellorship I used to meet the faculty each term to discuss University development, although it was a sign of the times – and not a happy one – that academic development increasingly figured less than other matters at these meetings during the 1970s. I also welcomed and did as much as I could to extend our early leavers' scheme, which brought students, often excellent students, without two A-levels to the University, and 'Town/Gown' links, although I did not like that term. I was very proud of the University's Arts Centre which was named after Lyddon Gardner, our benefactor. Indeed, the sudden death of Lyddon Gardner was one of the biggest blows to me as Vice-Chancellor. In time, he would probably have succeeded Sydney Caffyn as Chairman of Council. He enjoyed Sussex, as did Stella Reading, who also died suddenly and bequeathed Swanborough Manor to the University. They always wanted to meet undergraduates as well as members of faculty. Through them and many others the University of Sussex was always more than a University of Brighton. It was related to the whole area and it had a particularly strong impact on Lewes. It was never an ivory tower.

During my last years at Sussex national policy had a bigger impact on the academic pattern and on the mood than local factors. In December 1973 I described the delayed quinquennial settlement as falling short not only of our hopes but of our expectations: it was, I said, very difficult to live with. There were by then over 3500 students (3.9 per cent of them from Commonwealth countries and 8.8 per cent from foreign countries) and we were told that numbers of Science undergraduates should be pegged and numbers of postgraduate students reduced. There were then nearly fourteen applicants for every place in Arts and Social Studies and the research grants for the Science Area of the University totalled nearly £800,000. We had been remarkably successful in raising outside funds for research.

On the eve of the quinquennial visit of the University Grants Committee in November 1975 the latest annual recurrent UGC grant had fallen by 8 per cent in real terms, but the University was still in surplus. New capital monies, we were told on the occasion of the visit, were 'miniscule in relation to needs' – even this was an understatement – and we were asked to set lower targets – under 5000 by 1981–82. 'There is no immediate hope', the Chairman of the University Grants Committee explained, 'of the restoration of the quinquennial system.'

In my last years at Sussex we had to freeze all new appointments and pool whatever posts became available by reason of retirements and resignations. We were forced, therefore, to return from devolution to a greater measure of central allocation of funds. We were forced also to spend more time on trade-union negotiations – these, too, had to be handled centrally – and on counting the cost of our social facilities, like our residential centre at the Isle of Thorns. It was clear that the tasks of a Vice-Chancellor were changing, not only in Sussex but in all universities. The year 1974 was a landmark in national history. It was a year when no one could afford to be complacent.

I did not leave Sussex two years later in 1976 in order to go to Oxford. I had told my closest colleagues and the Chairman of Council, by then a very close friend, that I wanted to cease to be Vice-Chancellor after ten years. I felt that this was the right period. Before the announcement was made, however, I had been invited to return to Worcester College as Provost. I decided to accept the invitation. My last months at Sussex were among my happiest since the exciting beginnings, and a summer conference on interdisciplinary work in arts and social studies, arranged by some of my colleagues, seemed to me exactly the right kind of farewell. I returned to the preoccupations of my first years as administration passed into other hands.

It did not seem quite the right time to present my own account of what we had set out to do, and I am not sure now that this is the right time to evaluate it. Twenty-five years are less than the conventional span of a generation. A Vice-Chancellor's account can never do justice to all that was happening. The other essayists in this volume will not only add to my account: they may well choose to change it.

2

The Lean Years, 1976–1986

Denys Wilkinson

During the 1960s and early 1970s the purposes of the University of Sussex had been defined, and its fabric, material and intellectual, built up. All had been done well. When I came here in 1976 an academic institution of international repute for the novelty and quality of its teaching and for the success of its research in both arts and sciences occupied striking and attractive buildings sensitively set into a lovely fold of the South Downs. But already threatening handwriting was appearing on the walls of academic cloisters throughout the land. The expansionist bubble of the 1960s that had taken the age participation rate from 7 per cent in 1960/61 to 14 per cent in 1970/71, and had swept Robbins along with it, rather than been induced by it (so much for academic folklore) had mysteriously burst. It is still not clear why this was; why the age participation rate, after an unbroken and linear climb for a decade, suddenly flattened off and, indeed, then declined. Was it Vietnam and the ensuing 'student revolutions' and the flight from science that soured the atmosphere for higher education? Was it that primary and secondary schooling simply could not adapt itself to supplying qualified 18-year-olds at the increasing rate that the history of the previous decade insisted was possible? But for whatever reason, the projections of university expansion for the 1970s, made during the 1960s, proved wrong in the event. University funding, based on these false projections, was therefore excessive and we saw the embarrassing need to give money back to the Treasury.

The University Grants Committee had, in effect, lost its independence in 1964 when it became attached to the Department of Education and Science with the severing of its previously direct link with the Treasury. (It must be admitted that the Treasury had already begun rather firmly to question the advice that the UGC had been giving it and no longer simply handed over to the UGC whatever sums it was assured were going to be needed to nurture the universities in the coming years.) After 1970 there were little funds for continued expansion or new projects, developmental or capital. Neither were there takeovers such as had occurred in the UGC quinquennia beginning in 1957, 1962 and 1967, whereby funds previously supplied by the Research Councils were transferred from the Research Council in question to the UGC, in turn to be incorporated into the quinquennial grant. This shift away from takeover significantly reduced university income in the long term.

Added to all this there was an increasing financial pinch in the country as a whole; prosperity had given way to stagnation and inflation; everywhere economies were being sought and cost–benefit analysis began to be applied to activities, such as education, for which it is inappropriate. The quinquennial system collapsed and its revival has never been on the cards. By the mid-1970s universities were living from year to year, hand to mouth, often not fully knowing their money for a current year until that year was well under way or almost over. Not only was there no quinquennium on the basis of which responsible plans might be laid, there was not even a meaningful forward look to provide some sort of guidance as to our possible position in relation to Micawber's great divide. Arbitrary and irrational cuts became the order of the day. The only thing to cheer the universities' corporate soul was Lear's: 'The worst is not; So long as we can say, "This is the worst".' I have made all that sound pretty grim, and so it was and remains; Lear knew what he was talking about.

When I came to the University of Sussex in 1976 things had begun to look tough for the universities, although nobody then dreamed of what was to come. I came from Oxford where I had been for 19 years building up what by the time of its completion in 1971 was Oxford's largest science laboratory. Everything came on the expansionist wave that brought UGC and Research Council money almost on demand. But by

1976 the tide had turned and it was obvious that the ensuing years were going to be a battle against that tide that was bidding fair to take away much that it had brought. This was very much on my mind when Sussex asked me if I would like to be considered as its next Vice-Chancellor. I realised that at Sussex also things would be tough financially and that retrenchment would be more likely than expansion but there I should be able to take an overall balanced view and would not feel that I had to defend my own at the cost of others whom I knew to be as deserving as I. And so it has been.

The nine years that, as I write, have passed since my arrival, and the year that will have additionally passed before our Jubilee, have been, and will be, very hard – harder by far than I could have imagined in 1976. They have not been so much the lean years of my title as the leaner and leaner and leaner years. Problems have increased in severity as time has passed; no sooner has one begun to take stock than another shock has been forecast or felt. We certainly do not yet know our terminus.

I am no historian, as the rambling sketch that I have just given amply demonstrates. But I know how synthetic history can be; I do not want to trust myself to chronicle those years afresh when I have, in large measure, already recorded them in my *Annual Reports* to Court. I shall therefore trace the years, with their threats and blows, and with the ripostes made to those threats in extracts from those *Reports*, lightly edited. If it seems a tale of apprehension and foreboding, that is because that is what it was and what it remains. But through it all the University of Sussex remains in scholarship and research at the very front of the field and with its cherished principles of teaching as bright as before. I shall not refer to one of the great determinants of the 1980s and 1990s, namely the demographic decline, nor to other major unresolved balances, such as the binary line and the various faces of rationalisation, nor to domestic matters however important.

The academic successes of the University in its short life so far have been little short of staggering. In acclaimed publications, major prizes, named lectures in both arts and sciences we have been resplendent. In the 'league table' of non-UGC income we have been in the top three, together with Oxford and Cambridge, ever since records have been kept. In the latest listing of Science and Engineering Research Council science funding we were, *in terms of absolute cash*, third only to Oxford and Cambridge, even though we are classed both as 'small' and 'arts-based'; we received more such money than the bottom dozen universities put together. The last time I did the sums we had six times the national average of Fellows of the Royal Society (half the universities of the country have no FRS; we have had 17). We have had more Fellows of the British Academy than all the other 18 post-1960 universities put together... And so it goes on, and must go on despite the dismal chronicle that I am about to unfold.

1976/77

This year will be remembered as the one during which the embattlement of the universities of this country forced itself upon general recognition. The 2500-year-long honeymoon that started with Plato's Academy is really over; in future, higher education, in particular university education, will be required more and more to justify itself in terms of its cost-effectiveness and its social relevance, and can no longer rely upon simply being thought to be a Good Thing.

The universities are now being asked: 'What are you for?' 'Surely,' government argues, 'if the universities are as vital to the well-being of the country as they would have it thought, their protests will articulate their purposes in the way that we and society, to which we are responsible, can understand.' I should, in fact, feel less uneasy than I do if I believed that government, indeed, got as far as thinking like that before squeezing; but whether it does or does not, the situation remains the same: we now know that unless the universities can put up what I might term a reasoned howl the squeeze is not likely to be relaxed.

It is absolutely right that we should have to think rigorously about our purposes but I should believe it to be wholly wrong were to be called upon to justify our activity *in toto* in quantitative terms of cost-effectiveness. Society is not static and its true needs are not narrowly to be determined and quantified; as important as vocational accomplishment is the ability to recognise the general structure of the problems that life throws up, and to relate those problems the one to the other – what we might dub intellectual technology transfer is tremendously important. Training in intellectual rigour, in openness and receptivity, in ability to identify, simplify and solve a problem – these are the things that distinguish a university training, training for quality of mind, from a narrowly vocational training. The universities have evolved in response to needs that have been real but which have not been articulated except through the belief in the Good Thing. I have elsewhere this year had occasion to write of the universities as 'having evolved organically ... forming a kind of intellectual ecology that will be disrupted only at the nation's long-term peril'; this I hold very strongly.

1977/78

Last year I wrote of the increasing demands that are being made of universities to explain themselves and their purposes. Universities are also coming under other sorts of pressure, some of them building up so rapidly that it would be foolish to attempt a summary at the present time. Whether good or bad in themselves, these pressures are leading to a progressive erosion of something that we have always held dear: university autonomy. The pressures of legislation, whether or not accompanied by the increasing impact of unionisation on university management, have led to a progressive centralisation of a whole range of university determining mechanisms. Centralisation, in itself, implies some loss of autonomy and, once again, this is not necessarily wholly a bad thing. But, good thing or bad thing, all this needs closely watching and demands close analysis. It is certainly not to be hoped that the university system of the nation will totally change its structure but that structure must show itself able to move with the times.

1978/79

Financially, we began the year with some increasing hope of a longer planning horizon than had been possible in recent years. However, all that is now water that never even got to the bridge. All our expectations have recently suffered dramatic modifications. The changes came with the change of government during the summer of 1979; the new government being explicitly committed to a policy of economy in respect of public expenditure. Precisely what effect these economies will have upon this University is not yet clear, but it is likely that effects will be most profound. We expect that for the academic year 1979/80 there will be a cut in real terms of about 3 per cent, and that in the following three years funding will be no better than level in real terms. A gloss of tremendous importance lies in the concomitant decision on the part of the government relating to the long-vexed question of overseas students. The government has now taken the draconian step of deciding that in making its awards to universities it will simply subtract from the notional level funding in real terms the total economic cost of all overseas students now on course. This amounts to about 16 per cent in the case of the University of Sussex. In other words, the income to the University from the government is going to be reduced by about 16 per cent over the next three years, and we shall have to ease this shortfall by charging whatever fees we decide upon to such overseas students as will come and pay them.

The case for having overseas students in UK universities is a well-known and overwhelmingly strong one and if it were not totally justified, as it is, in terms of the direct academic, social and cultural benefits brought into our universities by overseas students it would be justified on the narrower grounds of national self-interest since it may be cogently argued that the 'subsidy' to overseas students, that would be represented by charging them just the same fee as is chargeable to home students, is more than recovered, in the longer term, through economic benefits to this country associated with the ex-overseas students' knowledge of it and by the goodwill and influence for us that the ex-overseas students carry when they return home. The government's policy is doctrinaire, ill-considered, shortsighted and a betrayal of our obligations to those most in need. Every effort must be made to bring about a reversal of this extreme policy, the consequences of which could be so far reaching and devastating.

1979/80

Last year the government declared its intention of putting the university system on to level funding by which it meant that it intended to maintain the value, in real terms, of its total funding less the sum that it had subtracted on account of overseas students. However, in October, the University Grants Committee asked all universities for an estimate of their student numbers in 1983/84 on the basis of three hypotheses. Even on the most optimistic hypothesis we are in financial trouble with a deficit of 4.2 per cent against existing commitments; on the most pessimistic hypothesis our deficit becomes 19.2 per cent.

The envisaged financial losses, at the upper end, were so great that severe staff losses would be entailed and very substantial academic damage sustained. Faced with such a possible disaster situation the University set up a small working party, consisting of the Chairman and Vice-Chairman of Council, the Vice-Chancellor and Pro-Vice-Chancellor [the Area Pro-Vice-Chancellors and the Chairman of Education were added later] to carry out a deep study of all aspects of university expenditure in relation to academic and non-academic activities. This party, the Group to Review Income and to Plan Expenditure (GRIPE), has not yet issued any final report and its only significant conclusion is that academic as well as non-academic activities would have to bear a share of the privations in order to minimise the overall damage. Unless there is a major turn-up in the fortunes of universities, to rely upon which would be blindly irresponsible, we shall be faced with severe academic and human problems; no matter how severe they may be, we must find ways of sustaining the vitality of our academic body politic for without development and without fresh blood, we should wither.

1980/81

The storm has been gathering for some years. We now look back upon 1979/80, when major privations to come were already writ large, and when government support of teaching and research was already in serious decline, as the halcyon days. November 1979 saw the official announcement of the government's policy towards overseas students. But at that same time the government assured us of level funding in respect of the rest of our academic economy. All that is now swept away by genuine and admitted volume cuts which conspire with inadequate compensation for inflation and with the increasing cost of staff on salary scales, to face us in 1983/84 with a shortfall of more than 20 per cent relative to the forward projection of our 1980/81 baseline. The storm has broken.

GRIPE has worked continuously for the past two years and has now published a major report that recommends in full, illustrative detail what the shortfall of 20 per cent must mean. The effects on the University of so large a contraction in so short a time must be extremely severe; the time involved, only two years, is totally incommensurate with natural academic and managerial timescales. The government's policies cannot but severely damage the university system; the consequences for the professional, industrial and business life of the country, let alone the devastation of academic and intellectual activities, could well be disastrous. Continuous representations to government have brought no response and we must fear for the very understanding of those upon whom our heritage depends.

But come what may, I am determined that the University of Sussex must win through as the centre of excellence in teaching and research that it is now recognised to be; we must preserve and build on our strengths and in confronting the agonising human problems of the coming years, with understanding and with compassion, we must nevertheless recognise that our major responsibility towards staff and students alike is towards future generations and towards the University of Sussex that will emerge from the period of anguish into which we are now plunged.

1981/82

Our present perspective was defined by the now famous, or notorious, July letters of 1981 in which the UGC gave the universities of the country their slices of the reduced cake and which faced us with an effective reduction in income in real terms of 21.5 per cent as between 1980/81 and 1983/84 (following which level funding is once more promised). A cut of this size cannot be handled as a perturbation; even if its across-the-board distribution were right, which it is not, it could not be effected by normal managerial mechanisms because the very substantial reduction in staff demanded could by no means be achieved by natural wastage and normal retirements particularly in faculty categories.

GRIPE made its initial full report on 6 October 1981. All spending units submitted their suggestions by early January 1982; they were considered by GRIPE and assembled into a University Plan that was discussed by the central committees and approved by Council on 5 February 1982. Since that date we have therefore had a fully agreed target towards which to work, distressing and discouraging in the extreme as that task may be in both academic and human terms. We oppose the cuts and shall continue to do so; we deplore the academic and human damage; we lament the frustration of the aspirations of youth, but until the upturn comes, as surely it must, we must do our best with the resources that are to be allowed us and on that course we are now firmly embarked.

There is a danger that the 20 per cent rundown may become an end in itself so that we begin to speak of 'success' in its achievement and forget that that 'success' implies grievous loss. I hope that we shall not fall into such a way of thinking; a bad job made the best of yet remains a bad job, and 'the cuts' are a very bad job indeed.

It was quite clear that for academic faculty there was no chance of achieving the 20 per cent reduction without special methods. These were agreed by government in January 1982 both in respect of early retirement for older staff and voluntary severance for younger staff. As a result of the availability of these mechanisms some 30 of the 65 losses needed by 1983/84 had been achieved by 30 September 1982. Our ability to avoid any form of compulsion is being greatly helped by the admirable gestures of many academic colleagues in taking periods of unpaid leave; we recognise a debt not only to the colleagues taking the leave but to the rest of the subject group whose load is thereby increased. Voluntary departures, while moving us towards our target shape in the most managerially 'painless' way, are by no means painless in other respects: senior colleagues, highly respected and valued, are being lost to the University with considerable damage; both teaching and research are inevitably suffering and extra strains are being thrown on those remaining. We are in a position of delicate balance both financially and academically but spirit and morale, given the circumstances, are splendidly high and it is to the immense credit of the University, having recognised and responsibly faced the most serious problems, that this is so.

1984*

Our slow and painful adjustment to the great cuts of 1981 continues. The damage to our efficiency and effectiveness of operation has been considerable and it is likely that some of that damage, particularly in relation to the loss of technical staff, will not be fully manifest for some time.

During the autumn of 1983, further significant clouds have appeared upon the horizon. The first is the suggestion from the Secretary of State for Education, in a letter dated 1 September 1983, that universities may not assume (despite the promises of 1981) that level funding will be forthcoming (following 1983/84). The second cloud is a request from the government to consider increasing our student intake by about 8 per cent without any extra cash apart from the fees associated with each student, which themselves amount to only about 10 per cent of the cost per student.

The cumulative effect of these uncertainties has been further compounded by the University Grants Committee's announcement, in a letter dated 1 November 1983, of a major consultative exercise on the development of higher education to the end of the present century. The letter poses 28 questions, some of them going to the very heart of the university system. The effect of these continuing uncertainties and the

---

* *Annual Reports* are now dated by the following calendar year.

gnawing attrition of cuts, either sudden or creeping, make proper planning, particularly for academic developments, difficult or impossible.

A welcome development has been the recognition by government that the effective standstill in academic faculty recruitment had deprived the universities of one of their most precious assets, namely young active academics on whom the future well-being of an institution so largely depends. The provision of these New Blood and Information Technology posts to the various universities was on a competitive basis. At Sussex we succeeded in getting four of the New Blood posts on the Science side, which reflects favourably on our consistently high research activity, and we secured three posts in Information Technology. Although this New Blood money is precious and welcome it also represents a direct influence exercised by government, through the Research Councils and the University Grants Committee, on the academic balance within universities and might therefore be regarded as an infringement of proper university autonomy. This effect will be closely watched.

1985

The grand inquisition of the university system in the form of the 28-question examination paper set by the University Grants Committee on 1 November 1983 has come and gone. Have we passed? We do not know. The Secretary of State has so far responded only very incompletely; his chief message was a reiteration of his wish to see better and more socially-relevant higher education at lower cost. The Green Paper that will chart the proposed course for higher education towards the twenty-first century is awaited in 1985, and then we shall know more. Shall we see reefs and shoals that will be no more than an extension of the obstacle course that we have been negotiating for the last several years, or shall we see the dim looming of a new continent? We do not know and there is little point in guessing, but a few disturbing facts and trends are already emerging.

Judgements of balance and need can be made only by the

universities themselves. In effect to threaten to remove that right and duty from universities not only obviously strikes at the holy cow of university autonomy (a beast that, in my view, it would do no harm to rouse from time to time with a few good whacks) but, more importantly, reveals an insensitivity to, and a lack of understanding of, the nature of the close-knit academic fabric out of which universities must by their very nature be constructed. We in the University of Sussex are particularly vulnerable to this type of attack because of our avowed attachment to interdisciplinarity and, in particular, because of our cherished Contextual teaching which makes it essential to preserve a broad spectrum of expertise even at the cost of some numerical (not qualitative) thinness of its individual constituents.

Another point of concern is the UGC's call for a clear definition by individual universities of research strategies, on the basis of which it will make selective distribution of the research element of its grant. Concern attaches at a number of points: the articulation of a research strategy necessarily entrains the making explicit of domestic judgements as to strengths and so, at least by implication, as to weaknesses that may be better left to our normal processes of resource allocation and that may be unhappily divisive if effectively published; it is difficult to reconcile the UGC action with the present concept of the dual support system; the UGC's intention is clearly interventionist and may be thought to display a too close interest in the detailed working of individual universities, little short of infringing their autonomy.

The old order is changing with the rapidly increasing interventionism of the UGC in universities and of government in the UGC already foreshadowed in the New Blood scheme to which I referred in last year's *Report*; perhaps it is indeed the looming of an unknown continent with the winds of change blowing strongly towards it. If so, we must not pretend that the new continent is not there or try to tack away from it back to a position that has gone for ever; universities are now too expensive, and the reasonable calls for the demonstration of their social relevance are too insistent, for us to hope, or even wish, for a return to the almost unquestioned boom quinquennial economy of yesteryear. It is our present job to ensure that government understands the nature and purpose of universities and their vital contribution to the well-being of this nation through the provision of a well-educated citizenry, understands their delicate, vulnerable and close-textured academic structures, understands their problems of balance and long-term planning and understands that they cannot be factories that can be programmed to turn out as many of this or that sort of graduate to order and can switch from one to the other at what is, in terms of the ineluctable timescale of academic processes, a month's notice. If the unknown continent is looming we must ensure that we are given what we need to explore and exploit it to the benefit of all, including particularly, as I am sure we are well placed to do, the University of Sussex.

1986

This *Report* has not yet been written but it will tell of the publication, in June 1985, of the long-awaited Green Paper that was no more than a rehash of previous calls by government for more and better for less; it will tell of the UGC letter of 9 May 1985 instructing universities to submit, by 30 November 1985, plans for the years through 1989/90 on the assumption that their income will decline by 2 per cent per annum in real terms; it will tell of the details of the bidding exercise for UGC research funding that, in effect, puts 30 per cent of UGC grant at risk. It will tell of the UGC's call for greater internal discrimination within universities, for their establishment of performance indicators and for their setting-up of associated mechanisms for the distribution of research resource including academic faculty posts. It will tell of the UGC's intention, by May 1986, to indicate to universities their quantitative expectations for the rest of the decade in students and cash, although that longer horizon will itself be highly provisional and in no sense a return to the assured funding over a significant period of the vanished quinquennial days.

THE FUTURE

My story of these ten years has not been a happy one; it has been peppered with expressions such as 'arbitrary and irrational cuts', 'threats and blows', 'apprehension and fore-boding', 'embattlement of the universities', 'ill-considered, shortsighted and a betrayal of our obligations', 'far-reaching and devastating', 'very substantial academic damage', 'disaster situation', 'severe academic and human problems', 'devastation of academic and intellectual activities', 'agonising human problems', 'period of anguish', 'frustration of the aspirations of youth'. I have doubted in my *Reports*, and I continue to doubt, whether government understands what universities are for and how they work; but, as I said in my most recent *Report*, it is our job to make them understand; it is up to us to do it. In my very first *Report*, at the beginning of the ten lean years, I wrote, truer than I knew, 'unless the universities can put up what I might term a reasoned howl the squeeze is not likely to be relaxed'. We have not managed that reasoned howl; we must try harder.

The continuous strains of contraction and retrenchment of the ten lean years have not yet stayed the quite dazzling flow of scholarly products for which this University now enjoys so wide a reputation in so many fields, both arts and science. To some degree, however, this continuing flow represents the momentum of earlier years; present privations are eating at the seed corn. But the talent and spirit, in teaching and research, remain tremendous and must surely be recognised, even by an unhappily blinkered government, as a precious national resource. One day, although it would be hopelessly irresponsible simply to sit back and wait for it, there will be a turn up for the book: we shall be ready.

3

Student Perceptions of Sussex

SUSSEX PIONEERS
Michael Kenward (1963–66)

Mud, snow and optimism. Not the usual elements of a university's academic reputation, but the stuff of memories of a Sussex pioneer. For the University's academic community, the 25th anniversary is a time to review academic achieve-- ments, and to see where the University stands now. For those of us who were the University's earliest undergraduates, 40th birthdays probably mean more than 25th anniversaries, but both events are cause for thinking about the past as much as the present, prompting a stronger bout of nostalgia than usual.

For all undergraduates, the time spent at university should be a time of excitement and discovery. But there is inevitably something special about being a pioneer. If nothing else, the fact that buildings were rising around us, and that courses were being run for the first time, added something special to undergraduate days. There was more than that to the excitement of Sussex in the mid-1960s. The first under-graduates were part of a new wave. Sussex was not just a new university, but the first of a series of new universities. In these times of academic gloom, it is difficult to recall the heady days of the 1960s when the new universities were laying the foundations for an era when a university education would be available to anyone capable of benefiting from it.

Participants in any drama are likely to exaggerate the importance of their role, but in those early days there were plenty of signs that the audience too was interested in the events on stage. How many undergraduates today have been the object of intense curiosity, rather than morbid interest, among the media? In the 1960s, reporters and film crews were regular visitors to Falmer House – about the only bit of the campus that was presentable – and they came not just to visit the famous Jay twins. (Media attention reached its most embarrassing in an appearance on *Look at Life*, a strange 'educational' interlude inflicted upon cinema audiences of the day.)

At the time, the excitement spread beyond the boundaries of Sussex. The world, including Britain, was going places. The future was to be with the young. The faculty were young – sometimes not much older than the students. Unemployment had disappeared, for ever, in the 1930s. Many of us thought little about finding a job until final exams were upon us. You chose your job: it didn't choose you. A degree, any degree, was a meal ticket for those who wanted it.

The academic construction of the University went hand in hand with the physical construction. Piles of mud and bricks were bound to affect the lives of the people who had to pick their way over duckboards and dodge construction machinery. If nothing else, each new term brought new buildings into action, making it difficult to know where to go. One of the greatest changes came when the library suddenly became the bar and, with its makeshift shelving removed, appeared to double in size. (It could probably hold – and perhaps sometimes did – a quarter of the University.)

It isn't all nostalgia and concrete-mixers that come back after more than 20 years. Something of the academic tone of Sussex in the 1960s still sticks in the memory, although it wasn't all excitement and innovation, perhaps because a new university has to bow to conformity in some matters if it is to establish its reputation among a sceptical academic community. For example, today's undergraduates would probably be surprised by the conventional way in which the University assessed its students. Exams dominated the process. Of course, there wasn't room then for many people to sit exams on site: the ballroom of the Grand Hotel, the Polytechnic and a new boys' club in Kemptown all brought a new excitement to exam time.

While the exams seemed very conventional, there were

other sides to the academic life. Some of these 'add ons' were more in tune with 'the Sussex experiment'; but while some undergraduates may have enjoyed them, no one seemed to pay much attention to them when judging performance. This may have been just as well; my third-year research project in physics consisted mostly of moving a laboratory. (Funnily enough, this turned out to be more typical of the life of a working scientist than contrived experiments.)

Another project that appealed to some, but probably bored others, was the Arts/Science Scheme. Every undergraduate had to cross the dividing-line to see something of how the other side lived. There were lectures: Asa Briggs on history for Science undergraduates, John Maynard Smith on biology for Arts students, not to mention physicists. There were even projects. But this turned out to be one of those ideas that died (at any rate for Arts undergraduates) when the enthusiasm of the early years faded. Some members of faculty clearly had little time for the Scheme – meetings cancelled, projects not returned, let alone marked. Oddly enough, the Arts faculty, usually reckoned to be more interested in events beyond the ends of their noses, showed less interest than the scientists and helped to kill the notion that every undergraduate should participate in the Scheme. On the other hand, perhaps the experiment revealed its influence in the graduates that came out of the University in the early days. It may be the circle I inhabit, although the 'official' news of alumni tends to confirm my impression, but the number of Sussex graduates in the media, where it helps to be able to straddle the two cultures, seems to be higher than you would expect.

The mood of the 1960s did not last long. Recession soon came along. (It is easy for an early Sussex graduate, or any graduate for that matter, to believe that life has been one long economic recession since graduation day.) As a result, universities went into decline under governments of all persuasions, and were in no position to recruit new members. Employment prospects for graduates have dwindled; undergraduates now show greater enthusiasm for the straight-and-narrow of their subject – not for them time 'wasted' on peripheral activities, no matter how stimulating they may be to the intellect. From the outside, it looks as if those early optimistic days were a temporary aberration. Or is that remembered optimism just nostalgia brought on by 25th anniversaries and 40th birthdays?

SUSSEX REFLECTIONS
Tony Baldry (1969–72)

Sipping coffee in the outworn Edwardian splendour of the *Brighton Belle* one approached Brighton station. All around streets of trim terraced houses stretched towards the sea. It was because of the sea and its proximity to London that the Prince Regent had bestowed his patronage on the small fishing village of Brighthelmstone soon to become Brighton. Ever since this royal endorsement by the Prince Regent, Brighton has been a seaside town – a slightly risqué, slightly eccentric seaside town, but definitely a seaside town with piers, pierrots, promenades, pebble beach and picture postcards.

It was to be at a spot between the deckchairs and the Downs that Sussex University sprang forth in the early 1960s. The spirit of learning, seaside air, Spencian architecture and 1960s excitement had combined to create a university of which Anthony Sampson in his 1965 *Anatomy of Britain* could write 'most popular University of all, most competitive for places ... friendly and sophisticated'.

By 1969 there was no self-consciousness amongst Sussex students of in any way being new. The University community was confident, self-assured and on the whole quietly deter-mined to achieve academic standards that would stand com-parison with any other university in the country. New students arriving at Sussex University in 1969 were expected to spend their first year either in one of the then three halls of residence on campus or in one of the seaside guest-houses available off-season for students, or in private lodgings. The majority of freshers went into either one of the guest-houses – the Montpelier, the Regency, the Hotel Cecil, the Squirrels and many, many more – or into lodgings that were spread throughout the town; this also meant that Sussex students were spread throughout Brighton. Thus unlike some other university towns there was no university quarter in Brighton;

the whole town was part of the University and the whole University was part of the town.

Sussex students studied in Schools of Studies a Major subject in the context of the broader disciplines of that School. For me it was Law in the context of Social Sciences. Such an approach made our university courses fuller, wider and more rounded. To this day I am still using notes from my Preliminary statistics course to help me evaluate the welter of statistics that have become required reading for every politician.

There were invariably complaints that the Contextual subjects bore little relationship to one's main subject, but as they were invariably interesting in their own right this seemed not to matter too much. On glancing recently at my finals papers taken some 13 years ago, I found the Law questions to be surprisingly easy but some of the Contextual papers I would today now find it difficult to respond to – *Concepts, Methods and Values* in the Social Sciences BA final examinations of 1972 contained questions such as:

> If social theories are merely ideologies in Karl Mannheim's sense (i.e. merely a function of the generally prevailing social situation) is there any point in trying to assess their factual validity?
> And: Discuss with examples the status of probabilistic laws – can empirical enquiry settle the holist–individualist controversy?
> And: Are there transcultural standards of truth or rationality by which to judge concepts, beliefs and practices of societies?

I am reasonably certain that having once grappled with the holist–individualist controversy, even if only fleetingly, has helped prepare me for more immediate problems such as trying to understand Treasury funding of local government and the Rate Support Grant system!

University life at Sussex was rich and varied with numerous different activities and sports frequently carried out to very high standards. However, the activity which tended to attract the most publicity and attention from the media and the rest of the world was student politics. Even at the end of the 1960s, the heyday of student activism, student politics at Sussex was generally a minority interest. Sussex students were not apathetic about politics, just about student politicians. The national political parties all had a small core of supporters, and then there was an assortment of left, broad left, Marxist and far left groups all competing for student support. Union general meetings tended to be mainly boring to all but the most committed and were thus ill-attended. Students' Union pronouncements tended thus not to reflect the views of students as a whole, but were portrayed as such by local and national newspapers. One candidate for election as President of the Students' Union concluded his address at the election meetings by taking down his trousers – it was a hard act to follow and he was duly elected!

There was an overwhelming sense of optimism at Sussex in the late 1960s and early 1970s: graduate unemployment was not then a reality so the overwhelming majority of students were confident in the knowledge that they would get their degree and a job in due course. There was an optimism that tomorrow was always going to be slightly better than today, and a seemingly inherent self-confidence among Sussex students that by their energies and efforts they could and would influence tomorrow. In subsequent years since leaving Sussex, meeting those who were contemporaries with me at University, I have been reassured to discover that little of that optimism has evaporated.

THE EVOLUTION OF A STUDENT
Harry Dean (1972–77 and 1977–78)

The fact that I am now, some nine years after graduation, able to express some of my warm feelings about my days as a student at Sussex is, in itself, a form of praise for the University. For, when I arrived at Falmer in October 1972, still four weeks short of my eighteenth birthday, I was absurdly unprepared for what was to follow.

During the preceding summer holiday I had imagined a wonderful, glittering world where I would be instantly recognised as the lovable genius I believed myself to be. I had anticipated reclining in the library and dreamily putting the finishing touches to another scholarly piece of work before strolling across campus for an early evening drink with other, like-minded souls. And I longed to be immersed in the endless series of exciting things that would surely occupy every available minute of my free time.

I was after all going to be a student at *the* new university where academic ideas and political new dawns were eagerly discussed into the early hours. This was certainly the view of my teachers who had desperately tried to advise me on my choice of universities. They saw Sussex as intellectually excellent but very frantic and a bit odd. It was a kind of educational black hole into which young academics disappeared, trapped for ever by an unimaginably strong force field of radicalism. As I was entering for a degree in the School of Biological Sciences I often wonder what they thought Arts and Social Studies were like.

Not surprisingly my imagined world failed to materialise and I was soon languishing in the small, shared guest-house room in Kemptown that was my first non-parental home. There was nothing wrong with the guest-house. In fact, the landlord was a delightful man and a living refutation of the dictatorial stereotype often associated with such individuals. The other residents were also a rather splendid bunch, although thirteen young males under the same roof tended to encourage certain eccentricities in behaviour and lifestyle.

The problems arose whenever I ventured forth from this relative security to enjoy the meaningful experiences that three years at Sussex University were meant to provide. Nothing I tried seemed to work. I did a great deal of 'participating' in tutorials and seminars which, in my case at least, meant talking a lot without having done the necessary reading. Nobody, least of all my tutors, seemed terribly impressed. The other spheres of student life that were meant to buttress my academic progress were no more rewarding. I became involved in Union politics but found to my great shock that I was surrounded by people infinitely more articulate, confident and well-informed than myself. Even my attempts to prove that a Science student could benefit from a well-rounded interest in all things was a disaster. I still remember with horror stumbling, bleary-eyed, from the Brighton Film Theatre after watching four Pasolini films without a break. The intensity and interest with which the other masochists were discussing the significance of it all was a humbling experience. Culture was clearly not for me.

The overall effect was fairly disastrous. My interest in

academic life began to wane and a crippling loss of confidence made a hermit's existence look quite attractive. I was firmly convinced that Sussex University was a hostile environment in which the weak could only wither and die. The idea of leaving began to take root and it was only a deep-seated fear of failure that stopped me from bowing out of the struggle for survival.

Then, slowly, things began to change. Perhaps the most tangible development was that, to my astonishment, some of the people I first met through my Union and political interests began to turn into friends. The realisation that they too were often struggling to come to terms with their first year at university liberated me from the worst aspects of feeling inadequate. I think I was particularly fortunate in meeting those people but I also believe very strongly that Sussex was the sort of place where, unless you were very unlucky, an individual could thrive and develop.

Once I experienced the feeling of belonging to a group of friends it became easier to make sense and enjoy the benefits of the University as a whole. I soon realised that Sussex *was* an exciting place with almost limitless opportunities where social evolution was a more appropriate concept than survival of the fittest. The key to it was that instead of expecting to be the passive recipient of automatic fulfilment and entertainment I had to exploit actively the potential that was there in many, different forms.

My new confidence led to a renewed enthusiasm for the affairs of the corporate student body which resulted in a fascinating and enjoyable year as Treasurer of the Students' Union. During that sabbatical I thought long and hard about my academic frustrations. Apart from realising that some hard work might be a good idea, the most important change was that, with the help and encouragement of some of my tutors, I transferred to the four-year Biology degree in Cultural and Community Studies (CCS).

Despite the easy ridicule of some of my friends at a Biology degree that allowed a course on science fiction (albeit as a Contextual) I am convinced that the CCS degree (later renamed Human Sciences) represented all that was good about the interdisciplinary ideas on which the University was founded. There were frequent criticisms of the structure of the course and its lack of integration from some quarters of the University but I loved every minute of it. My interest was maintained and refreshed by the differences in subject-matter, approach to teaching and modes of assessment between the science and arts components of the degree. I was also lucky enough to receive support, inspiration and considerable informal supervision from the tutor most responsible for maintaining the degree in increasingly difficult circumstances. He has since left and is, I believe, living in Cumbria. I sometimes wonder how symbolic his departure was at a time when all the talk was of Sussex becoming more conventional and less innovative.

Although it took five years to obtain my degree, rather than the three on which I had originally planned, the extra two years were the best investment of time I have ever made. Even my traumatic first term was well worth the suffering and I feel very privileged to have been a student at Sussex.

A LOVE AFFAIR WITH SUSSEX
Victoria Bourne (1977–81 and 1981–83)

I was warned that Sussex University would be very windy, and that it was also a hot-bed of Marxism. I arrived there somewhat tentatively therefore, but standing in the fields above the campus, gazing down at the fantastic Moonbase which appeared to have accidentally landed there, my love affair with Sussex began. This was where all my questions would be answered, and I would find peace.

Some of my contemporaries began packing their bags no sooner had they found themselves living on campus, their main criticism being that at best, it was like living in an office, never being able to escape work and go home, and at worst they were imprisoned, cut off and isolated from the real world. The same reasons were behind my affinity with the campus. It was a paradisical dream-world, with its own laws and beliefs, multiracial and harmonious, usually non-sexist and non-violent. It was a pleasure to escape the world for those years and work in the intoxicating, timeless atmosphere, where the amount of hours in each day was irrelevant and we could actually choose the stage at which we would work, eat or sleep. We had all the time we needed.

As for being cut off from the rest of the world, I had never felt less so than after my year abroad in Moscow, when I would await telephone calls every Sunday morning from my Russian boyfriend, on the pay 'phone in the tunnel between the bookshop and the coffee shop.

Sussex gave the space needed for a practice run for life itself. We could experiment in all areas, intellectually, socially and spiritually, and there was room to make mistakes with no far-reaching effects – just plenty of time to try again.

Campus had as many moods as a person and the changing faces of thousands of students over the years seem to make no difference to these moods; the character of the campus remains the same, regardless of who passes through it. In summer it was covered in blistering heat, resembling an intellectual holiday camp, with students lying on the grass, using their Short-Loan library books as pillows. On bright, blustery days in the spring, it felt as if the sea was lurking immediately behind the library; there were stormy, black days, with the driving, horizontal, unique-to-Sussex rain which made it a feat of human endurance to get from the library to the refectory. Campus was illuminated by great, winter sunsets and at night it was full of mystery, promise and excitement. Campus also once showed a new and unforgettable face: sitting in the half-light of the desk lamp with my revered Russian tutor on a winter evening as we discussed *Anna Karenina*, it became bathed in slow, heavy snow, and we both fell silent to watch.

In the final year we all longed for the end of the take-away examinations so that we could enjoy all the freedom of Sussex with no work to bind us. The days were spent in the library until nine o'clock at night, with frequent coffee breaks among all the debris of empty plastic cups and newspapers in the EURO common room, and were followed by nights in East Slope Bar, or dancing away the tensions in The Crypt. But when the end of the examinations came, without the work we found only a huge, desolate gap, and we enjoyed ourselves somewhat desperately in an oppressive vacuum.

Sussex had certainly been very windy, and yet I cannot say

that I met more Marxists than any other type of person. But it was definitely a hot-bed, of thought, analysis and discussion. As Sussex graduates continue to seek each other out all over the world, the University's strength is clear: these people are easily recognisable by their reluctance to accept anything too quickly and their questioning minds. They know enough to realise that they need to know far more and are constantly thirsting to find out, with real love. Thankfully, my mind will never find that peace I had hoped for. Sussex did not answer any questions for me; it only taught me how to pose more.

ANOTHER SUSSEX HIPPY BITES THE DUST
Nigel Savage (1980–85)

To my parents, with love and thanks for seeing me through nineteen years of full-time education.

The first year at Sussex I lived in 24 Park Village (24PV). In many of the houses on campus students seemed to live very atomised lives, in which people on the ground floor didn't know those on top, and vice versa. But 24PV was not like that. Right from the start the twelve of us were a proper household, and though we all had other friends we also socialised together. We practised our cooking skills on each other, learned to tolerate assorted spouses of varying degrees of permanence, and generally got down to the business of living for the first time in a shared house.

The experience of living in 24PV dominated my first year and, to some extent, my whole Sussex career. In fact it seems to me now that if a historian had to assess which part of the University had the greatest influence on students' lives it would not be a particular School or tutor, but rather the humbler souls in the accommodation office. If Chris had not been a residential adviser in Katy's corridor I would never have met her; if Caroline had not been placed next to Bill in Holland House she would not now be living in Massachusetts; and so on.

Of day-to-day life at Sussex memory blanks out the routine in favour of the highs and lows. So I remember the time we went for dinner at Woodfords and ended up skinny-dipping on the main stretch of beach. I remember the great victory parties we had at Food For Friends in successive years on election night in the Union. I remember seeing the Irish World Cup squad train at the University in 1982, and I remember Steven Berkoff's *Hamlet*, at the Gardner Arts Centre in February 1981, as one of the finest productions of anything I have ever seen anywhere. But I think also of the pain of ending relationships as well as the pleasure of starting them, and of what it feels like to be barracked as a politician as well as applauded. I remind myself of the extraordinary loneliness possible in the middle of a busy university. And I remember Marcus Simkins, who died in a car crash and who was as gentle as he was huge, and Debbie Graystone, who drowned off Cornwall, and whose memorial service in the Meeting House was as upsetting as anything I have ever attended.

Of my happy memories a disproportionate number seem to be set in Stanmer Park. I think of walking over the hill, late on a frosty moonlit night, when the church and the graveyard seemed eerie and the pond was frozen and we fed the ducks; or running in the summer when there were cricketers playing on the green outside Stanmer House, and the Americans always thought it so English. I remember the night in January 1985 when there was very heavy snow, and I joined a huge snowfight outside Essex House; and then later, after midnight, I remember four or five of us pinching a shower curtain from Norwich House and taking it over to Stanmer to use as a toboggan; and later still trudging back, tired and happy, and settling in for hot chocolate and Scotch.

The best night of all in Stanmer was in June 1983 when we put on *A Midsummer Night's Dream*. SUDS (Sussex University Dramatic Society) had decided to do the play at the Gardner Arts Centre as their summer production, and were already in rehearsals, when I suggested to Colin Herrman that it would be fun to do the play in its natural setting – in a wood, close to a graveyard, on midsummer's eve. He and I spent a fun afternoon in Stanmer declaiming Shakespeare to see how far our voices carried, whilst a series of dog-walkers and local residents, passing by, confirmed all their best prejudices about the eccentricity of Sussex students.

The actual performance turned out more wonderful than I think any of us had expected. The cast was superb, the audience was happy (it was the end of term the next day) and the play itself was perfectly suited to its setting. When the lights were first switched on, just after nightfall, people really gasped, audibly, and applauded at the sudden beauty of our main oak tree, centre-stage, all lit up in reds and blues against the woods behind and the night sky. For the final scene of revels in Athens a bonfire was torched, and after the play ended we stayed by the fire, entertained by a lone flautist, until dawn. It was the stuff of which clichés are made, and we loved it.

Listening to a flute by a bonfire in a public park in the middle of the night was not, however, a typical Sussex night out. And even if it had been, it still would not have been the sort of experience which, in the long run, could have changed me in any way. Yet Sussex definitely left its mark on me, and it is for leaving its mark on me rather than for specifically good times or bad that I will remember Sussex the most. I spent my third year in full-time office as Vice-President of the Students' Union, and I spent the year after that studying in Washington DC, and by the time those two years were over my interests and beliefs had definitely shifted.

In the Union I was part of the mainstream for most of my first year. I got onto the Union executive in about my fourth week at Sussex and stayed sufficiently out of trouble that when I was elected chairperson of the Union, six months later, my nomination form was signed by the leaders of all the major political groups on campus including both the anarchists and the Tories, a Sussex record of sorts.

I didn't manage to maintain such bipartisan support, however. I was elected chairperson in time to chair the last big occupation at Sussex, in May 1981, and the consequences of that, together with the Union's foreign policy pronouncements at the start of my second year, were enough to leave me permanently disillusioned with the Sussex Left. From then on I always knew which side of the barricades I was on, and so did they, and that knowledge added a certain zest to my year as Vice-President. Moreover, I was Vice-President with specific responsibility for the Union's finances, and the day I took office the Union had debts of £35,000, no cash, and no friends in either the bank or the University's administration. I was twenty at the time, and it staggers me now to think that I should have ever wanted to get into such a position, and certainly I had a predictably crazy year. But I survived it and, more remarkably, so did the Union's finances. I now know that it was a good year for me, even if at the time it didn't seem particularly enjoyable.

Politics is a minority sport at Sussex, and I doubt that it figures in the memories of many students. But it was a sport in which I participated from the start and so it dominates my own memories of my time at Sussex. In the end I left Sussex most conscious of the paradoxes of my university career. I never thought when I arrived that I would leave despising the Left rather than a part of it; nor did I think that my general indifference to religion would become an affirmation of my Jewishness; nor did I anticipate that a vague interest in American politics would become a deep fascination with American history. In a University thought to be made up of rebels, the thing I rebelled most against was a part of the University's culture itself. By the time this is published I should be wearing a pin-striped suit and a new pair of cuff-links. Another Sussex hippy bites the dust ...

4

The Impact of the University on the Local Community

Brian Smith

A few years ago I organised a survey in which 300 adult residents of Brighton, Hove and Lewes were interviewed in their homes to determine the extent to which local people normally had contact with the University, had met staff or students, or were even able to distinguish between the University and other educational establishments in the area.

The results are difficult to summarise briefly, but as might be expected, age and social class were predominant factors in determining response. Overall, 98 per cent of the sample claimed to have heard of the University, 90 per could describe its position accurately, 43 per cent had visited it for some purpose, 37 per cent knew a member of staff or a student personally, and about 15 per cent had what could be described as positive and on-going contact. It also seemed clear that the most common reason for visiting the University was to attend a performance at the Gardner Arts Centre, and that most interaction with University members was of a 'social' rather than an academic nature.

Since the University started in 1961 it has grown from a tiny group of 52 students and ten faculty meeting in two hastily acquired houses in Brighton, to the present 4500 students and 2000 employees occupying buildings at Falmer which, together with their contents, are now worth more than £100 million. What kind of impact has the University had on the area, bearing in mind particularly that expansion was rapid and for the most part took place during the first few years?

Some facts are relatively straightforward and can easily be established. As the third largest employer in the area and one that has brought a large number of young people into the community, the University during its brief existence has had an effect on housing, employment and the general economics of the area. The impact of the Gardner Centre, the Centre for Continuing Education and other obvious points of contact can also readily be evaluated, at least in terms of the number of functions organised and attendances at them.

More controversial, and certainly harder to assess, is what might be described as the emotional relationship between the University and the community in which it finds itself. As in so many human relationships, first love was followed by a period of disillusionment. More recently there have been encouraging signs of reconciliation. An intriguing question concerns what lies in the future – separation, or a partnership based on a more realistic set of mutual expectations, increased tolerance and understanding.

Housing has always been a live issue locally, and a common complaint from residents has been that the presence of the University has increased the strain on accommodation. In Brighton it is commonly believed that students occupy flats which would otherwise be available to families, and in Lewes one estate agent has gone on record as saying that the presence of the University has added 10 per cent to the price of houses. Both assertions are only partially true. However, there is no doubt that by the end of the 1960s students were adversely affecting housing provision in the area.

The original guest-house scheme, in which first-year students occupied Brighton guest-houses during term time, was creaking to a halt, but the supply of new campus accommodation was inadequate to meet growing demand. Housing statistics for that period underlined the need for action. According to the 1971 Census there were 60,315 households in Brighton of which 5850 lived in rented furnished accommodation. Assuming that the average occupancy was about three students per dwelling and 400 students stayed in lodgings, the implication was that about 670 flats or houses were rented to students, equivalent to about 13 per cent of the entire stock of furnished accommodation available.

Under pressure from residents, Brighton Council served notice on the University that it would withhold planning permission for future new buildings unless more rooms were provided for students on campus. The threat was unnecessary since the University was already committed to expanding accommodation on site as rapidly as possible. In spite of the difficulty at the time of raising the large amount of loan capital required, within five years student-occupied rented accommodation in Brighton had been reduced by one-third, or about 800 students. The proportion has remained fairly static ever since. Nowadays, it seems that students are frequently welcomed as tenants. But it has to be admitted that this probably has more to do with the belief that the provisions of the Rent Act exclude them from establishing tenure than a positive appreciation of their finer qualities!

Concerning staff, about 53 per cent live in Brighton which, taking student residence into account, implies that about 3 per cent of all Brighton households are University-occupied. The concentration in Lewes is higher, with an estimated 10 per cent of all privately owned houses being inhabited by University employees – the other large presence being East Sussex County Council. However, the main pressure on housing in the area comes not from the University but from the large general influx of migrants that has occurred during the past 20 years. The population of East Sussex has increased by about 15 per cent, with half of the newcomers already retired – about 28 per cent of East Sussex residents are now retired, compared with a national average of 18 per cent.

The presence in the locality of a large retired population plus many students has also distorted employment figures, so that the area is now characterised by apparent high levels of unemployment coupled with low 'activity' rates (85 per cent for men). Both students and the prematurely retired are of work age but for different reasons are unavailable for employment. Similarly, the ratio of unemployed to jobs available has remained low compared with other parts of the country which have much higher levels of unemployment. Education is categorised as a service industry and the economy of East Sussex is heavily biased towards this sector generally.

There is no evidence to suggest that staffing the University has affected local employment radically, either by attracting people away from other jobs or by otherwise distorting local supply and demand. About 56 per cent of all people in employment in East Sussex work in Brighton, Hove or Lewes, and 2 per cent of these are employed by the University. Most academics and highly skilled employees are migrants into the locality, and so far most have departed from the area when they have left the University.

The money entering the local economy due to the presence of the University can be estimated by means of a simple input–output model. For example, national surveys of family expenditure suggest that staff are likely to spend about 75 per cent of their income locally. Thus in 1985–86 £10 million will be fed directly into the economies of Brighton, Hove and Lewes from this source.

Students spend a significant amount of money locally, too. If we assume that in the current year all students receive and dispose of the equivalent of the full undergraduate grant of £1830 during their 30 weeks of term time, then after deducting the amount paid to the University for accommodation, catering, books, etc., a sum of £5 million remains which is spent annually by students, mainly in Brighton. The actual total is probably still higher because the above estimate does not take account of the postgraduate population who are in receipt of a larger grant and in residence all the year round.

To date about £60 million have been spent on land, buildings, furniture, equipment and library books at the University, and these investments are currently valued at £115 million. The annual recurrent budget for teaching and research is now in excess of £25 million, of which £20 million come in tuition fees and from the government in the form of various grants. The balance is donated by industry, foundations and other organisations to fund specific research projects.

An analysis of revenue payments made by the University during a recent period showed that 20 per cent of the total expenditure was on goods and services purchased locally. Making allowances for possible imbalances and scaling-up to obtain an annual figure leads to a sum of £2 million for the year, excluding payments made for utilities such as gas, electricity and water. Rates, rents and insurances account for a further £1 million.

These items, when added to the amounts spent annually by

staff and students, result in a grand total of £18–20 million for local expenditure per year. So the apocryphal 'disgusted' of Hove who writes occasionally to newspapers complaining that the University is 'a drain on the rates' is quite mistaken. On the contrary, the University makes a very positive and direct financial contribution to the local economy.

So much for housing, employment and financial considerations. But what about the educational impact of the University on the community? The general activities of the Education Area are described in another essay. However, the most obvious and sustained effort that has been made by the University to put its professional expertise at the service of the community has been through the Centre for Continuing Education, so it is appropriate for some mention of the work of the Centre to be made here.

It is interesting to trace its origin. The foundation stone for extramural work by the University was a paper presented to Senate in March 1966 by Asa Briggs. In this, he proposed that the whole University should share responsibility for such work because not only did many existing activities have extramural applications, but also extramural work was a two-way process which could enrich and benefit both University and community. Recognising that adult education in various guises was already well established in the locality, he suggested that the University should not enter the field to rival existing provision, but should aim to provide additional and complementary courses, especially in subjects where the University would be able to offer particular expertise.

Senate accepted the report, noting that increased contact between members of the University and the community would be valuable for many reasons, including the possibility that in the long run it would help diminish the gap between experts and laymen, and between graduates and non-graduates. It was also hoped that as the extramural programme evolved it would contain a research and development element, oriented to the present and future needs of the region. Among the activities that were envisaged were part-time courses for special occupational or vocational groups, assistance to voluntary and other agencies concerned with general community adult education, joint courses with the Open University, cooperation with local television and broadcasting, a University of Sussex Summer School, topping-up courses for Sussex graduates and pilot schemes in new subjects which the University considered to be of fundamental importance.

Because of the lack of UGC funds, the extramural programme was not launched until 1969, when the Oxford Delegacy agreed to transfer the responsibility for East Sussex to the University. The extent to which it has subsequently proved possible to implement the original ambitious plan has also been curtailed by limited resources. The main work of the Centre now falls into two categories – open community courses for the population at large, and post-experience, in-service education for various professional groups.

Open community courses are aimed at those members of the community seeking non-vocational further education. They are open to anyone over the age of eighteen and are neither examined nor assessed although students are expected to attend regularly, to read recommended books and to present written or other practical work under their tutor's guidance. In the session 1983–84 more than 4700 students enrolled in such courses, of whom some 75 per cent completed their chosen activities satisfactorily. They were able to select from a list of some 100 subjects which were taught at over 50 locations by over 130 tutors. It is worth noting that enrolments now exceed the total number of full-time undergraduate and postgraduate students in the University.

The other major activity of providing post-experience, in-service and professional training modules has also developed satisfactorily, given the limited resources available. There are courses for doctors, social workers, educational psychologists, magistrates and probation officers. These are largely self-financing and many involve the maintenance of on-going relationships and sometimes complicated negotiations with appropriate representative bodies, including local government and the TUC.

Those associated with the Centre for Continuing Education still retain a vision of 'continuing', 'recurrent' or 'lifelong' education as a central feature of future educational systems. Whether this will remain a dream during our lifetime is anyone's guess, but as Manny Eppel, the Director of the

Centre, pointed out in a recent report: 'Our descendants may look back in astonishment at our 20th-century tradition of enormous expenditure of money, human resources and skills on the education of a relatively narrow age-band of the total population.'

Impressive though its record undoubtedly is, when it comes to maintaining contact with the wider community the Centre for Continuing Education is not in the same league as the Gardner Centre, as became clear in the survey mentioned at the beginning of this essay. The creative arts were initiated at Sussex as early as 1962 by a grant of £48,500 from the Calouste Gulbenkian Foundation. The construction of the Gardner Centre was made possible in 1969 by a gift from the late Dr Lyddon Gardner. Designed by Sir Basil Spence, it has an auditorium seating some 450, an exhibition gallery and various offices and studios. The building has several practical drawbacks and space has always been under pressure, but in spite of these limitations many very successful events have been presented.

British universities do not share the American tradition of creative arts programmes based on the college campus. There are university-linked theatres of course: the Nuffield Theatre at Southampton, and the Northcott Theatre at Exeter are obvious examples. But the Gardner Centre pioneered the attempt to provide a comprehensive and professional university-based arts centre in this country.

The debate about what should be the proper objectives of the Gardner Centre would make good theatre in itself. Attempts to resolve the basic and probably unanswerable question – 'What is an arts centre?' – have been accompanied by a conviction that an arts centre associated with a university ought to have a distinctive character. It was agreed at the outset that the Gardner Centre need not, indeed, should not, compete with the commercial theatre that was available locally and at Chichester and London, particularly when Sussex has always prided itself on its ability to innovate and establish new traditions.

In 1972 the role of the creative arts within the University was reviewed and as a result two decisions were reached about the Gardner Centre, both important because they set the pattern for subsequent policy. The first was to confirm that the Centre was to be community-based and -oriented. To encourage this sense of shared responsibility, one-third of the reconstituted Gardner Committee, which was the body responsible for making major policy and programme recommendations, was drawn from the wider community.

The second decision concerned the programme balance at the Centre. Recognising that no two people were ever likely to agree as to which of the art forms should be given precedence, and that available talent and enthusiasm will inevitably fluctuate with time, it was decided to provide a facility that was flexible and able to respond to current needs, rather than attempt to define permanent and highly specific objectives for the Centre, which would have the effect of limiting its possible range of activities.

There have been many occasions on which the Centre has cooperated effectively with local organisations for their mutual benefit. For example, during the springs of 1972, 1973 and 1974, professional theatre groups based at the Gardner Centre visited local schools and presented plays which had been carefully chosen to encourage involvement by children and teachers. Such was the enthusiasm displayed by participants in 1974 that the tour, originally planned for two weeks, was extended to seven. At the time, East Sussex was the only county in the south without a Theatre-in-Education team and under more favourable conditions a more permanent joint venture might have been established. Unfortunately, however, the cold winds of change were already beginning to blow and in 1975 East Sussex County Council was forced to discontinue its backing because of financial cut-backs.

One notable achievement of the Gardner Centre has been the number of events that it originated that have then been successfully transferred elsewhere. *Ashes* by David Rudkin, starring Ian McKellen and Gemma Jones, and *Side by Side by Sondheim* are amongst such productions that were well received in London. It has been encouraging that not only have artists of the calibre of Timothy West and Dora Bryan been willing to play at the Centre but major London managements represented by Michael Codron, John Gale, Cameron Mackintosh and Patric Lau are happy both to send their touring productions to the Centre and to launch their new productions there.

On the music side, John Williams, the Boys of the Lough, the English Chamber Orchestra and the Academy of St Martin-in-the-Fields are amongst those who have given outstanding performances at the Centre and several groups of musicians have spent periods in residence. In early days the Allegri Quartet, and more recently the Chilingirian Quartet, have been particularly popular. With open rehearsals and regular return-visits, such groups attract an attentive and supportive following which adds greatly to the enjoyment and appreciation of performances.

Highlights of the exhibitions include a collection of photographs by Eadward Muybridge – sequences taken from the first ever motion pictures, produced by a dozen cameras, each with electromagnetically operated shutters and projected by the extraordinary 'Zooproxiscope'. An annual craft and textiles exhibition brings local craftsmen into the Centre each December. The outstanding event to date, however, must be the 'Drawings and Documents 1900–1930' exhibition, which included a remarkable collection of items from artists such as Vanessa Bell, Duncan Grant, Wyndham Lewis, Paul Nash, Stanley Spencer, Jacob Epstein and Roger Fry.

When the Centre opened in 1969 an independent organisation was launched – the Friends of the Gardner Centre – with the aim of furthering the active interest of the local community in the work of the Centre. Although small numerically, the Friends have often exerted considerable influence on the activities of the Centre.

Surveys at the Gardner Centre show that at most performances roughly two-thirds of the audience is non-University and people are prepared to travel considerable distances for events that they enjoy. Ballet and dance have proved increasingly popular in recent years. Response to the cultural diet is as might be expected – mixed. Comments such as 'The experimental lacks appeal although I appreciate it may be valuable for the young and is justifiable at a University' are balanced by 'Brighton is often a cultural desert ... much of the Theatre Royal programme is not my kind of theatre.'

As was stated at the outset, for many people the Gardner

Centre provides the only tangible point of contact between Town and Gown. In 1985, following another review of its activities, the University took the final logical step in handing the facility over to the community. The Centre is now run by an independent trust on which the University, East Sussex County Council, Brighton Borough Council and South East Arts are all represented. It will be interesting to see whether this more realistic sharing of responsibility by the wider community will result in a greater stability and a new spate of success for the Centre.

A recent innovation that must be mentioned is the Services for Industry programme. This was inaugurated six years ago and through it the University offers a wide range of product development, consultancy and advisory services, together with access to the most modern scientific and computing equipment, for industrial and commercial firms. Local companies subscribing to its regular information services now number more than 1000. In addition, a managing directors' club aims not only to bring local industry and the University together, but also to act as a forum for senior industrialists.

When Science Parks became all the rage a short while ago, the University made a conscious decision not to follow that particular route but to be more flexible, encouraging links with outside companies where joint interests existed. A good example of such a development taking place is the relationship that now exists between the University and Eurotherm International, a Sussex-based high-technology group. This company will shortly occupy a specially constructed building on campus that will house advanced design work for all the group's divisions. The intention is that Eurotherm staff will interact fully with the University's scientific community. One contribution that Eurotherm International has already made to the University is the endowment of a Chair of Computing Science, initially for a period of seven years.

There are several other points of contact between the University and the community which deserve to be described in detail, if only space would permit. These would certainly include the chaplaincy which, through its central ecumenical activities and its denominational groups, brings chaplains and laymen into contact with the University through organisations such as the George Bell Association and the Howard Society. However, it has always surprised me that so few people from local churches have availed themselves of the opportunity of hearing the outstanding preachers and speakers who have visited the University Meeting House over the years.

More exclusive in nature has been the Town and Gown club. This was originally the brain-child of Ted Shields, the first Registrar of the University, and Pat Rivett, Professor of Operational Research. It was launched in 1970 as 'an informal club at which members of the University and members of the Town might meet at fairly regular intervals over a meal to discuss matters of common interest'. Since then it has met regularly several times per year, usually at the University. When it started in 1970 many saw it as a bridge between Town and Gown when there was thought to be a considerable gap between the two. Its critics would suggest that in recent years it has become nothing more than a rather cliquey social gathering of the local establishment. However, it has served the useful purpose of introducing several hundred local residents to the University in a convivial and informal manner, and many of the evenings have produced educative and stimulating debate – surely one of several valid ways in which mutual appreciation and understanding can be fostered.

From the student viewpoint, community involvement has been high on the Union's priority list since the University began. The extent to which our students have played an active part in the Sussex Federation of Students' Unions and the National Union of Students has varied over the years, but their commitment to various local projects has remained consistently strong. Broadly speaking, these include helping the young, the old, the deprived and the disabled (or 'differently abled', as they prefer to call them).

Throughout the 1960s the so-called Community Action Group was run along similar lines to any other Union society. Fifteen years ago the Students' Union created a full-time post with specific responsibility for organising such matters. Dubbed Link-Up, and under the guidance of a Vice-President of Social Services, community action rapidly developed into the flourishing enterprise that it is today. The focus of its youth activities has been help given to running the adventure playground in Moulsecoomb. For several years an annual Kids Karnival has been held at the University and an annual holiday camp arranged for children from Moulsecoomb and Kemptown.

Students visit old people in the area, helping with shopping and housework, decorating houses and providing assistance with transport. A Christmas party has been given at the University for several years and is looked forward to by many regular clients. Link-Up also is active with the handicapped and the mentally ill. Frequent visits from student volunteers to St Francis Hospital aim to keep patients in touch with the outside world. Students also lend a hand when social evenings are held, and occasionally provide transport for day-trips to Brighton.

More controversially, Link-Up has become involved with various social action groups in the area, such as Tenants' Advice Services and the Women's Centre. Inevitably, some of these activities are disapproved of by sections of the general public, but it is unfair that such people are equally dismissive of all contributions that students make to the local community.

It is student activism, of course, that has caused the greatest strain between Town and Gown. The burghers of Brighton, having acquired their sought-after University, soon discovered that students did not necessarily share their views about life. Exposed to successive manifestations of youth culture and a vigorously expressed concern for various causes that sometimes went beyond the bounds of acceptable behaviour, Brightonians became distrustful of the institution that they themselves had successfully campaigned into existence. The sense of grievance is understandable – 'Why doesn't the University deal with these demonstrators, anarchists, etc.?' But what appears to the outsider to be simply a display of delinquency that ought to be countered by swift retribution is more often a complex situation, fraught with hazards, as many an unhappy University official has found to his cost.

Immediately following any incident public outcry reaches a crescendo and the University comes under enormous pressure to act precipitately. But the Vice-Chancellor is not an old-fashioned headmaster, and summary justice that does not carry the confidence and support of staff and students is likely to lead to crisis. A university has no police and has to rely on internal community support if disciplinary procedures are to be effective. At Sussex, in spite of what our critics might think, both the University and the Students' Union as a whole have always supported free speech and have been prepared to enlist all reasonable procedures in protection of it. When its fundamental ideals are threatened by a minority group the University needs support and understanding from the Town, not blind criticism. There are encouraging signs that such a sensitivity now exists and will continue to develop in the future.

The extended adverse publicity given to such incidents by the media has led to the suspicion within the University that the press is basically antagonistic towards it. If this is true then its effect on the Town perception of us must be considerable. I am frequently struck by the fact that nearly everyone I meet holds a view about the University, regardless of the existence of first-hand contact. When pressed, the *Evening Argus* is most often quoted as a source of information, closely followed by *Radio Sussex*. The *Sussex Express*, the *Mid-Sussex Times* and *Southern Sound* are also quoted. To check on possible bias I examined local newspaper coverage of the University during its lifetime, relating published reports to the events that took place.

As expected, *Argus* reporting has followed, or perhaps formed, local opinion. The euphoria and civic pride evident in the early 1960s gave way to bewilderment and indignation during the period of student revolt. Bad rather than good news has always achieved greater prominence, with student activities in one form or another achieving the greatest coverage. Relatively little space has been devoted to academic events and distinctions.

To what extent has reporting by the *Argus* been balanced and fair? Presumably newspapers publish what they assume their readers wish to read. About half of each issue is concerned with one-off items, including some national news. But the paper is mainly devoted to local issues – the deliberations of councils and organisations, and the activities of well-known characters and dignitaries. Thus a photograph of the Mayor of Brighton performing his civic duties appears as regularly as clockwork, and news involving both the Borough Council and the University understandably achieves some prominence.

Analysis of articles shows that reporting is generally neutral and fair with extensive quotations from all concerned. It is only the form in which items are presented which sometimes could be criticised. For example, during student rag week in 1975 the then Mayor of Brighton, Danny Sheldon, demanded that the rag magazine be banned on the grounds that it was obscene. Trying hard to be impartial, the *Argus* printed a lengthy rebuttal by the student organiser – but under the banner headline: 'Students Defend Filthy Mag'.

My favourite *Argus* report appeared in 1975 when Kit Kelly became student President. 'In black leather gear, jackboots and dark glasses, he seems a cross between a cowboy and a ton-up kid', commented the *Argus*. 'But that is as far as the image goes. Far from riding into another bout of student militancy, he is quietly assessing the situation and is seeking mutual respect between students and the town.' Later in the summer the World Association of Girl Guides and Girl Scouts held their conference at the University, attended by Princess Margaret, an occasion marred only by an unofficial demonstration from a small group of students. Once again it was Kit to the rescue: 'It was an amicable protest,' he was quoted as saying. 'We are really quite delighted to see the Guides.'

There have been periods when a more regular diet of information about the University has been presented by the media. For a year the *Sussex Express* carried a feature entitled 'Student's Notebook' which typically reported and commented on four or five items concerning the University each week. The *Argus* also carried a weekly column featuring the University from 1969 to 1972. But the prize for the most sustained attempt to explain the University to the wider community I claim for myself. For the past six years, with the help of Ken Whittington of the University Media Service Unit, I have presented a weekly programme on *Radio Sussex* called 'Ideas in Action', in which members of the University and others

63

associated with it have described their activities to the lay audience. Although the impact of these broadcasts on the community is presumably small, nevertheless they do constitute a unique University–radio cooperative venture and provide a further bridge between Town and Gown.

In case it should appear that I place the blame for poor public relations between the University and the community entirely on the media, let me emphasise that in my view much of the fault lies with the University. Our attempts at public relations over the years have been sporadic in effort and uneven in achievement. There are several reasons for this. Universities as organisations can be curiously diffuse and are sometimes not very adept at apology or explanation, because nobody sees it as his particular responsibility. Universities also suffer from a weak sense of corporate identity. Academic faculty, administrators, other staff and students all tend to view their institution from different perspectives; and even within these groups there is often a lack of shared assumptions as to what should constitute immediate priorities and ultimate goals. If we are confused no wonder others find us hard to understand!

Some academic faculty members, particularly perhaps those who are totally dedicated to their research programmes, regard the relationship between Town and Gown as largely irrelevant. Others see no reason why they as individuals should feel responsible for the University, merely because they happen to work there. Universities are also national and international institutions. Academics therefore belong to peer-groups that are national and international rather than local. Unlike schools, technical colleges or even polytechnics, only a small fraction of the student body usually originates from nearby – about 8 per cent in the case of Sussex.

However, in spite of the above disclaimer, I am delighted to say that all the evidence points to University members entering wholeheartedly into the life of the communities in which they find themselves. In an extensive study carried out a few years ago, I collated information supplied by 200 schools, 75 churches and 200 other local organisations of all kinds. In addition, over 1100 University staff completed a questionnaire giving details of their involvement in local affairs.

The Impact of the University on the Local Community

It is clear that University staff are linked with virtually every type of club, society and other organisation in the area. Forty-three University members act as school governors, eight are lay preachers, four are councillors and numerous others are active in local politics of every hue. Taking the academic faculty: they are twice as likely to belong to a political party; four times as likely actively to support a music, dramatic or cultural society; and three times as likely to belong to a civic society compared with the population at large. Church-going is on a par with the national average, social welfare groups are well supported, but relatively few belong to social clubs.

An incident occurred during my investigation that I found quite encouraging. One parish council refused to supply information about University involvement in its activities on the grounds that to do so would propagate the myth that University people are 'different'. For this council at any rate, University members really had become fully integrated into the community.

The University of Sussex exists today largely as a result of a successful campaign by local residents. Over 800 professionally qualified people have moved into the area to take up employment and these have become very involved in community life. Many cultural, civic, political and religious organisations have become revitalised because of the commitment of such individuals. Contributions by units such as the Gardner Centre, the Centre for Continuing Education and Link-Up have been described. However, there is one further fact that ought to be acknowledged – the extent to which the University has put Brighton on the international map. In many parts of the world Brighton is known, not as a holiday resort or a seaside town, but as the site of a distinguished university.

Town and Gown still have much to discover about each other, but it seems that mutual appreciation is growing and the will to learn exists. Surely, our vision for the future must include a desire for even greater understanding and cooperation.

5

A Challenge for the Humanities

Margaret McGowan

In 1961, the creation of a new university in Sussex offered unprecedented opportunities for the study of the science of man – his modes of thought; his powers of understanding; and his ability to create, especially with words. Twenty-five years later, those centres of enquiry are still as essential and still enthusiastically pursued at all levels, although the nation now seems less aware of their importance and is less generous in its support.

At the beginning, the humanities dominated thinking about 'the new map of learning', and helped to construct systems of study which laid great stress on the individual human growth of student and teacher, and which provided for a balanced experience of academic work. Thus, disciplines were to be studied within a broad cultural and historical framework of cognate subjects; work in depth was to be extended and enhanced by its larger setting; and the challenge was to create structures in which different disciplines could meet, learn from each other and cross-fertilise. Of the nine original academic appointees, eight were trained in the humanities; of the first three Deans, two were historians (Asa Briggs and Martin Wight), and one a critic of literature (David Daiches), who was sympathetic to history. It seemed inevitable that the humanities would make a strong mark on the future of the University and it is not surprising that they still play a significant role.* That role has none the less changed over the years. The transformations are attributable in part to new intellectual needs which have arisen from within the Schools

---

* There are four historians, for instance, on the present Arts Deans Committee, the executive committee of the Arts and Social Studies Area Committee.

of Studies, and in part to the readily perceived necessity to respond to educational pressures exerted from outside.

This essay will attempt to trace for the humanities some of the major shifts of emphasis and to describe those activities which have retained or strengthened their first aims and forms. It will try to give some flavour of the more recent ideas and preoccupations that concern us, and finally it will give voice to future prospects.

Those who come to study the humanities at Sussex in the mid-1980s, will become part of a large enterprise: 100 members of faculty engaged in teaching and research; about 1000 undergraduates majoring in one of the following: American Studies, Classical and Medieval Studies, English, History, Intellectual History, History of Art, Linguistics, Modern Languages (French, German, Italian, Russian), Music or Philosophy; and something over one-third of the graduate population in Arts and Social Studies. Although the humanities are spread across all five undergraduate Schools of Studies, they are particularly concentrated in three – the School of English and American Studies (ENGAM), the European School (EURO) and the School of Cultural and Community Studies (CCS; which grew out of the School of Education in 1970). It will immediately be observed that the organisation of academic work continues to be via Schools of Studies which remain a distinctive feature; indeed, Schools have proved remarkably resilient. Their academic advantages were well articulated at the start and many of these remain as cogent today. Multidisciplinary frameworks provided flexibility for growth and interchange while avoiding the isolation and inherent static condition of many traditional departments. For example, new disciplines have grown out of old ones – Intellectual History, Linguistics and Artificial Intelligence – and, however small, they have flourished in the larger School context. Others have combined – Philosophy with Literature, for instance – to create a closer interaction between two subjects. Such novel academic possibilities have been noticed and the interdisciplinary venture represented by a School of Studies has grown less unusual as time has passed, since it has provided a model for organising the arts now used in several other university institutions.

There are (and were) dangers present in such structures, however. Such frameworks made from a blend of several disciplines, which themselves continue to evolve and to grow, can encourage a loss of cohesion and even a loss of identity; and such a possibility appeared even more likely at Sussex when the common ground originally imposed on all Arts students through compulsory Prelims such as History and Philosophy was seriously modified. In fact, as the true consequences of these intellectual shifts were perceived, and as new disciplines called for their own kind of support, it became necessary to reconsider the nature and content of the School courses. In the late 1970s, therefore, each Arts School undertook a fundamental review in order to assess the continuing value of what it offered in the new circumstances. The process was begun in 1976 by the European School and was completed by CCS in 1981. Whatever the changes (some of which, in so far as they touch the humanities, will be discussed below), some things remained intact. Courses were transformed, some were deleted, and courses from additional disciplines were incorporated. Sometimes, as in the European School, the entire Contextual frame was rethought and recast. And yet, the School structure was not questioned. Thus, assumptions about the academic value of providing a wide context in which to study individual disciplines, and convictions about the rich fertility of Contextual courses *per se* prevailed.

Permanent, too, stands the merit of tutorials, or small group teaching as tutorials have become with growth in numbers of students and with a now relatively static teaching faculty. Small groups of three or four provide an informality between teacher and student which has itself proved to be infinitely precious for the humanities, whether it is in the exploration of a literary text, or in the arguments about methods and ways of presenting the facts that preoccupy historians, or in the patient probing of moral concepts and philosophical assumptions that underlie our mental habits or our attitudes to societies other than our own.

If one takes an Olympian view, small group teaching conceals the divisions and the debates that often lie at the centre of our intellectual concerns; these go on none the less in often highly individualistic ways in the tutorial itself (perhaps too much so), where students and teacher get to grips with their differing views and their varied approaches to different branches of knowledge. It is difficult to overestimate the benefits of this mode of teaching which relies on well-trained, gifted, enthusiastic teachers and highly motivated students. Its virtues have been rehearsed many times: the openness and flexibility of mind which it fosters; the questioning awareness; learning how to weigh material judiciously; and, most of all, that spirited independence which comes from the cut and thrust of argument. Less extolled, I think, and possibly of greater value, is the sense of involvement one gains from such encounters, and especially the enjoyment that comes from a sudden and shared discovery in a well-known text, or from an original thought sparked by the interchange of ideas from students studying diverse disciplines. The experience I describe is unusual. In the humdrum of many tutorials it may come rarely; but it does come, and it is a vital ingredient in the forming of personally mature beings. Of course, such a mode asks for a good deal of initiative and assumes a well-developed sense of independence especially from the student who – in the humanities, at any rate – has to spend many hours in the library, if he or she is to make the most of what we offer. Over the years, colleagues in the library have collaborated closely with teaching faculty to build up a collection of materials and of books (over half a million now), and to provide information retrieval facilities on which the student can rely to extend his or her knowledge. The tutorial experience has, in recent times, occasionally been supplemented by lectures, though these are still comparatively rare at Sussex except for Contextual courses where they perform a particular function. Seminars are more frequent since they provide a forum for students to expose their ideas to a wider audience and to develop those skills of criticism and articulation so necessary in the world in which we live.

The individual strengths which we try to encourage are also reflected in our system of assessment. In the Arts Area, the Preliminary examination was abandoned in 1972 (although Preliminary courses have been maintained); it seemed then an unnecessary milestone to those who define education as involving study and individual development disengaged from any need for continuous assessment of performance. The final examination attempts to evaluate the range of skills acquired through a variety of forms; some are traditional and others are more innovative; essays of 2000 or 5000 words, dissertations (10,000 words), projects involving a practical or creative dimension (for example, in Music), are combined for all students with three-hour unseen examinations.

It is now time to look at the progress of individual disciplines in the humanities. From the start, two subjects were given a privileged status: History and Philosophy. All students coming into the Arts Area were compulsorily exposed to both disciplines in the Preliminary course, and in two of the original Schools of Studies these subjects were required Contextual courses. The strategy which gave them this prominence seemed well founded; in order to equip students for a range of activities in the modern world, it was considered essential to develop their critical awareness, and their skill in argument. The study of history gives a sense of the past and more importantly perhaps is designed to investigate concepts, hypotheses and assumptions, to form analytical techniques and to scrutinise critically the nature of evidence. Philosophy, in another mode, develops similar talents. The University's first Prospectus (1961–62) expressed it this way: the study of philosophy reveals 'the diverse but connected ways in which language is used for different purposes in different contexts' and helps students to recognise 'the diversity of human thinking and the methods employed in different kinds of study'. Although the notion of such integrated work for all students is without doubt intellectually attractive, today it seems a somewhat old-fashioned way of redrawing the map of learning. The original strategy could not have properly taken account of the accelerated growth throughout the 1960s and early 1970s; it had ignored – necessarily – the need for a balanced array of subjects and the impossibility of achieving this if historians and philosophers had to be recruited in large numbers at a time when other disciplines required support; and, more especially, it had not anticipated the particular foundation needs of newly established social science subjects. The idea of a common course for all was, therefore, gradually transmuted as courses such as *Languages and Linguistics, Computers and Thought, Economic Analysis of Social Problems* and others were introduced alongside.

And yet it would be wrong to underestimate the continuing strength of history both as a discipline in its own right and as a crucially important intellectual training in a wider sense. In itself, it is a multidisciplinary subject and, in recent years, there has been a marked widening of the range of historians' concerns to include, for instance, an increased use of quantitative techniques and computer-aided methods. History continues to provide a natural context for many other courses; in fact, it permeates other courses and influences methodological approaches in younger disciplines such as Art History. Most disciplines at Sussex, at some time or another, have welcomed an historical perspective on their own concerns – for example, International Relations, Economic History and, to some extent, Sociology. Also, as we shall see, History provides an important component in many Contextual courses. Within the History Major itself which straddles all five undergraduate Schools, the initial pattern of study which was laid down has been sustained – namely, the preoccupation with three kinds of historical endeavour: the integrated study of change over time in a specific society; a broad topic in Comparative History; and a special subject study in depth using original materials. As the interconnections between teaching and research have always been close, it is not surprising that the most significant publications, in both quantitative and qualitative terms, have been inspired either by early traditions established within the Major – the emphasis on nineteenth-century Social History or Modern Political History – or by the School base – for instance, in the European School, work on the French Chouannerie, on occupation and resistance in France during the Second World War or work on German history in the Wilhelmine period.

Philosophy, by its nature and its present concerns, appears to have become more fragmented; certainly, diversification reflects its activities at Sussex. Within the Contextuals of all Schools of Studies, and indeed within the Major itself, Philosophy offers a rich range of options which are diversely taught by tutors. This approach, at once individual-based and

71

protean, has been the cause of quite radical shifts of direction which have probably been made easier and more speedy by the multidisciplinary structure which the Schools of Studies provide. On the one hand, Philosophy has linked up with other cognate disciplines to form new areas of research and teaching; and, on the other, fissures have occurred within the Major to create entirely new subjects. While the common interest in the study of language quickly bound together Philosophy and Linguistics soon after the latter had been introduced in 1978, the earlier strong literary interests of ENGAM had encouraged what was to become a popular combination in that School – a Major in Philosophy and Literature.

Some would argue that the Contextual pattern in Schools of Studies where the humanities are dominant (for instance, ENGAM and EURO) has close affinities with the history of ideas and that the continuing influence of History and Philosophy is still to be seen in these two Schools specifically in that context. Their influence can also be perceived, however, in the creation, in 1969, of a Major in Intellectual History which has become a meeting-place for the two subjects, drawing on the insights of related disciplines such as literary criticism, as well as methods implicit in the practice of philosophy or history. Although the study of Intellectual History is primarily based on the interpretations of texts by major thinkers and concentrates these days on work from the early modern period onwards, it is a demanding course for undergraduates. None the less, its successes in teaching and research are conspicuous, achieving international renown for published work in nineteenth- and twentieth-century social and political thought.

One of the most startling innovations to emerge, in part from philosophy and from the preoccupation with language among colleagues within it, and in part through association with other subjects concerned about the cognitive structures which underlie human communication (Linguistics and Psychology), is the discipline, Artificial Intelligence. Its particular character and the significance which we attach to this development is discussed in detail elsewhere in this book. It is nevertheless appropriate to observe here that what is generally

agreed to be a teaching and research area of supreme importance to the nation's health has its origins in large part in the
humanities, and in pure research interests on the activities of
the mind and in language.

In addition to the skills so far discussed, mention must be
made of the study of language and literature which, from the
very early days of the University, were recognised as having a
strong role to play. In order to enhance further the students'
critical and creative capacities, training in literary understanding and discrimination formed, and still forms, the basis of the
Prelim *Critical Reading* course in ENGAM – a course which is
also offered in CCS where understanding the individual and
modes of imagination are as essential to the work of that
School as the comprehension of social sciences such as Developmental Psychology and Sociology. In a parallel course in
EURO, characteristic modes of thought and feeling are
studied through the *Critical Reading* Prelim, which is based
on seminal works of the European imagination chosen to
illuminate moral experience, refine sensibility and illustrate
important conceptions of artistic form. The refining methods
of literary criticism and the acquisition of knowledge about
and experience of literary works of the past and of the present,
in all their richness and variety, provide the core to all literary
Majors. There are, however, particular characteristics of this
study of literature which are distinctive. In the first instance,
the study of literature is closely allied to its social, political and
intellectual context – the relations between the two have
developed in an unusually complex and adventurous way
inspiring the student to make original and unexpected connections, and encouraging interdisciplinary research of a high
order. Secondly, the creative impulse of colleagues and
students has benefited greatly from the emphasis on the
analysis of literary works, to the extent that it is not exceptional for novels and plays to appear side by side with critical
works from the same author commenting on creative writing.
Thirdly, since the early 1970s, eager and active interest in the
many developments in critical theory and in the dynamics of
reading has declared itself. This is an intellectually exciting
area of debate which, in graduate seminars, engages students
and faculty in sometimes hot exchanges, and results in publi-

cations which themselves become the subject of further discussion and analysis.

The close association of teaching and research is fully apparent in all the humanities. Yet, the indivisibility of these two activities can, perhaps, best be demonstrated either through the work of art historians or through the interests of members of faculty in the Music Subject Group. In both these areas primary research is founded upon teaching. For the Art History student, intense, technical specialisation as well as a breadth of cultural knowledge are required for an adequate grasp of the subject; this entails precisely the same kind of empirical, historical and technical research that has to be present when colleagues work on the exploration and reconstitution of art works from the remote or recent past, or in the tracing of larger movements of artistic consciousness and performance. In Music, too, it is increasingly difficult to disentangle commentary upon contemporary work from its actual production, since the study of Music, from its inception, focused on the contemporary scene; and this interest has been reinforced by the presence of gifted composers in the Music Subject Group whose compositions naturally attract talented students. The links between music-making, the sound resources of electronics and active public participation are well established; and they anticipate, and we hope will help to meet, the creative impulses and the performance needs which will weigh more and more in our society.

We have seen how, in the Schools of Studies, disciplines have worked together and blended to form new subjects. The agents which carry a heavy responsibility for such growth have been the Contextuals which have given a particular identity to each School and have provided a broad historical and cultural background which has informed, enhanced and extended the study of the Major discipline. Although Contextual courses have changed since the early 1960s, and some have disappeared (like *The French Imagination* or *The Russian Tradition*), and although incipient fragmentation has been checked by simplification and rationalisation, the cherished convictions concerning the basic functions of the Contextual have remained secure. Contextual courses that have grown and have endured like *Images of Childhood* in CCS,

Topics in ENGAM, or *European Foundations* and *Modern European Mind* in EURO and ENGAM, have done so because for both tutors and students they have provided opportunities to ask and to pursue all sorts of questions which had been artificially forbidden in the traditional syllabus. *Topics* in History or Philosophy and Literature, jointly taught by tutors from those disciplines, have encouraged students of literature, for example, not to move in simple chronological progression from text to text within some pre-set canonical tradition, but to be aware of the intellectual and social context of a text. Neither Contextual courses nor Schools of Studies have survived without criticism, and it must be a matter of continuing scrutiny that the latter remain fully responsive to developing educational needs.

Their robustness may perhaps be illustrated by some discussion of *Modern European Mind* (MEM). As soon as it was born, it aroused controversy. Originally designed as a background course for English majors, it soon gained the status of the key final-year Contextual in two Schools of Studies, EURO and ENGAM. Yet many tutors viewed it with profound mistrust. 'Superficial', declared some, disliking the false philosophic impression transmitted in the title that there can be such a thing as a mind of any period or place. 'Ambitious, immodest and impossible to teach', was the judgement of others. None the less, the grandiose title remained. MEM has generated an unusual response from students; persuaded the teaching faculty that a properly critical investigation of various modern 'prophets' who would exert influence whether we like it or not (Hegel, Marx, Nietzsche, Freud, Dostoevsky, Proust, Kafka...) was salutary, if not necessary; and even the most reluctant tutors came to regard it with enthusiasm as they discovered they could learn and teach at the same time as they tasted the excitement of shared discovery. The twice-weekly lectures which accompany this course have attracted colleagues to try out something original and this has resulted in outstanding publications – books on Freud, Sartre, Kafka, Hegel, and on ideology and art. Inevitably, the context of the course has not remained static; it has been modified to some extent to meet new academic developments within the School or within intellectual concerns at large – initiatives on modern critical theory, the reinterpretation of old questions concerning Marxism or psychoanalysis for instance, or the introduction of modern developments in jurisprudence. For the able student and for the teacher it remains an inspiring experience; for the less gifted it seems, and is, a daunting task. MEM thrives to a certain degree on keeping up-to-date with intellectual and literary movements, and since in the last 20 years or so these have been predominantly continental, English traditions have been neglected. It may be that in ENGAM, it has happened naturally that the American dimension should be emphasised through that bundle of options under the title *Modern America*; or it may be that the strong presence of European languages in EURO has fostered more detailed attention to the specifically European inheritance within the course.

Certainly, languages have flourished and they are by no means confined to language and literature degrees, although those academic interests have been strengthened by the recent introduction of integrated language degrees (French/German; French/Italian) which seek to exploit close cultural groupings within the European framework. All students in the European School study language; and whether their Major subject be Law, Politics, Economics or International Relations, they spend a year in a continental country studying these subjects with their European coequals. The value of linguistic skills associated with expertise in technical or vocational subjects has been extended to Science on the same principles. In this way, a strong awareness of belonging to Europe which marked the University from the start has been reinforced.

In this essay, from time to time, I have drawn attention to the fact that research and publication have often been directly inspired through teaching; and, although *The Idea of a New University* rightly and inevitably stressed the importance of undergraduate work, it was envisaged from the first that, as a University, it was necessary to develop graduate work and encourage research as rapidly as possible. Graduate students were first admitted in Arts and Social Studies in 1962; by the academic year 1965, they represented 20 per cent of the total student population, and in the current year, the same percentage make up the student body in the Arts Area and for whom a Graduate School was created in 1971. The rapidity in the rise in numbers reflects the paramount importance teaching faculty attach to graduate work and to research.

It is a difficult task to characterise adequately the research done here in the humanities. What one can say is that it is rich, abundant and diverse. Its range stretches chronologically from classical times to the present day; its variety extends from the long, sometimes painstaking establishing or creating of a text, to complex consideration of intellectual movements over time, or to the analysis and application of critical approaches to literature and ideas. As might be expected, the published work shows not only a sharp awareness of the context – past and present – which it seeks to explain, but also has frequent traces of the interdisciplinarity that comes from the daily rubbing together of ideas and methods from different disciplines.

Although considerations external to the University should make one cautious about predictions, it seems essential to venture some thoughts on the future for the humanities based on an assessment of what we have attempted and managed so far. I am grateful to colleagues who have most generously proferred their impressions which (with their permission) I have freely interpreted and used in this essay. But, as is customarily stated in the prefaces to books, I accept sole responsibility for what is written here.

It was an immense gift to be given the opportunity to experiment and innovate and to respond to the prevailing mood in higher education in the 1960s. That zest and vitality that gave the humanities a chance to develop in new directions are equally resolute today. The changes that have come to our courses derive from a readiness to consider seriously fresh needs, and to equip ourselves and our students to meet the challenges that could not have been foreseen. Powers of reflection and discrimination any student naturally confidently expects from a study of the humanities which relies so steadily on individual strength and initiative. Our approach also provokes enquiring minds, keeps them open and flexible, and eager to tackle bold careers. Specialists who are also educated people will be needed to play crucial roles in their many spheres where advances in technology now accelerate so fast. Our contribution to that advance has not been insignificant and, moreover, the study of the humanities has equal utility – as long as it is allowed to exercise its strengths – in ensuring that the human consequences of such technical progress are in harmonious balance.

6

The Social Sciences at Sussex

Donald Winch

When I came to Sussex in 1963, having begun my teaching career at Berkeley and Edinburgh, there were subtle differences between those who had been appointed in the first, second and third years of the University's existence; and while the faculty body doubled in that year, the place was still small enough for the differences to be fully noticed and nurtured. There are now very few people at Sussex who have lasted the whole course, and the differences have long faded into insignificance with time and expansion. I mention this because my main qualification for writing about the social sciences at Sussex is based on longevity rather than special insight or breadth of knowledge. Somewhat to my surprise, I find that I have spent the last 23 years teaching, first mainly Economics, later chiefly such Contextual courses as *Concepts, Methods, and Values,* in the School of Social Sciences. During that period I was also Dean of the School for six fairly eventful years (1968–74), a period that provided me with a liberal education in every conceivable meaning of the term. At that time I might have been able to lay claim to at least an academic administrator's overview of what is, after all, a very broad and amorphous group of disciplines concerned with the study of the various aspects of human life in society, wherever it is to be found.* But while we have probably done more than most other universities to cultivate the links which connect the various social science disciplines at all levels, to pretend that

---

* For purposes of this essay, the social sciences consist of Economics, Sociology, Politics, Social Anthropology, Geography, International Relations, Social and Developmental Psychology, Social Administration, Law and Urban Studies. I am grateful to many colleagues for information and advice, and would like to apologise for the limited use to which it has been possible to put that advice in what follows.

there is anything approaching a single common denominator would fly in the face of our own hard-won experience. The social sciences are still plural, and they have each arrived at their present state according to different timescales and via different cultural and historical paths.

Another daunting factor is the growth of the whole business. When I came to Sussex there was a School of Social Studies and Majors in Economics, Geography and a combination of Sociology and Politics, with plans to introduce Social Anthropology, Social Psychology and International Relations in the near future. But numbers were small, and only 20 per cent of Arts and Social Studies undergraduates (there were no postgraduates) were registered for degrees in the social sciences. Now they number around 1000 in all – nearly 50 per cent of the Arts and Social Studies total – with a further 200 postgraduates reading for higher degrees on a full-time basis, and an associated faculty body of over 90. Since most of this expansion took place in the early 1970s, it is entirely understandable why readers of *The Idea of a New University* get very little idea of how teaching and research in the social sciences have developed since the mid-1960s. But there is more to it than that: there are *no* references to the social sciences as a collective entity in that book – a fact which corresponds with my own early recollections of Sussex. The founding Deans on the Arts side of the University were all drawn from the humanities, and there was a tendency to regard the individual social sciences either as being essentially the same as the humanities, or as making contributions by way of analysis or empirical case-study methods to a scenario designed by and for the humanities. Those of us who were brought up as social scientists of one kind or another, and who were called upon to supply the initial text that would go under the various headlines provided by the founding fathers, had an odd task to perform. It entailed suspending scepticism, sometimes branded as narrow departmental-mindedness, about some of the territories to which vague labels had been attached, while discovering which of them were capable of supporting academic life on a more or less permanent basis. This must happen in all new institutions, but it was an especially acute and hence prolonged process in the case of disciplines whose special characteristics, whose outlines, whether hard or soft, had not been explored in any depth. In some respects there were more possibilities for fruitful collaboration between the social sciences than had been envisaged, in others less. But finding out which was which required a kind of second foundation, thinking anew in a context which accepted that over the last 200 years or so the social sciences have constructed a distinctive third culture of their own – one that is poised between the humanities and the natural sciences, yet retains close links with both sides. For this reason, and not merely, I hope, as a result of the bias created by my own experience, I shall begin by outlining some of the changes that were made to accommodate the growth in numbers of faculty and students with a professional commitment to the social sciences. And I shall do so by confining myself initially to the School of Social Sciences, the name given to Social Studies in 1970 to mark its predominant concern, as compared with other Arts Schools, with this third culture.

In the early years of expansion some effort was devoted to ensuring that Major subject courses comprised an adequate set. In some cases the laudable aim of establishing links between disciplines had been carried too far, with the result that Contextual elements had been included within Major subjects at the expense of courses needed to bring students up to accepted specialist standards, especially when laboratory, statistical, and field-work elements had to be accommodated. The original combined Major in Sociology and Politics was an early casualty in the process of reassessment. What might have been a suitable compromise for a more conservative institution wondering how best to accommodate Sociology, that sprawling and relative newcomer to the British academic scene, could not long survive the appointment of faculty whose training was confined to one or other of the disciplines involved. The phasing-out of this combination, together with the appointment of Professors of Politics and Sociology by 1968, was an important step in establishing the social sciences at Sussex on a proper footing. Equally important in this regard were the appointments to Chairs of Social Psychology and Social Anthropology, neither of which disciplines existed in most British universities at that time as single honours degrees, but for which Sussex was able to provide congenial homes in African and Asian Studies and Social Sciences. By the late 1960s, therefore, Sussex had acquired a representative hand of cards in the social sciences, though with some novel elements added.*

Changes were also made to Preliminary and Contextual courses. The privileged position originally enjoyed by History and Philosophy as Preliminary courses came under considerable pressure from numbers and the changing intellectual composition of the faculty and student body. It became harder to maintain that these subjects were the best, or only conceivable general points of entry into work at the university level, especially for those going on to major in a social science. In similar fashion, Economics lost its favoured position as the only social science on offer during the first two terms of a student's career. Alongside the original courses, therefore, many of the social science groups now mount courses designed with non-specialists in mind; and in adding to the list of initial offerings some significant innovations have been made which have proved capable of meeting genuine curriculum needs and of supporting research. A good example of this is the course *The Biological and Interpersonal Bases of Sex Differences*, where it has been possible at an early stage in a student's career to draw on biological as well as social and psychological perspectives.

Although such terms as inter-, multi- and cross-disciplinarity are frequently used in discussions of the Sussex pattern of undergraduate education, they have never been treated as self-certifying. Our practice when designing the curriculum has been as rarely determined by these abstractions as it has, say, by the Comtean aim of creating a unitary social science consisting of a hierarchy of disciplines with sociology at its apex. A more pragmatic approach has conditioned our deliberations. Thus some disciplines or subject areas, notably Social Psychology, International Relations and Geography,

---

* As an illustration of the shape of this hand, the Professors in the various subjects in 1968 were as follows: Tom Bottomore and Zev Barbu (Sociology), Marie Jahoda (Social Psychology), Tibor Barna (Economics), Tom Elkins (Geography), Freddie Bailey (Social Anthropology), Dick Hiscocks (International Relations) and Colin Leys (Politics).

are themselves inherently interdisciplinary in the most straightforward sense, having been formed out of elements drawn from what were originally separate branches of knowledge. Even the more professionally unified groupings, such as Economics and Social Anthropology, contain borrowed elements capable of being shared (or disputed) with other disciplines. No single formula could be invoked to cover all cases, and one early conclusion was that however open the boundaries of the different social sciences might be, however much they might be the product of historical and cultural contingency, they could not be treated as arbitrary. One obvious implication of this was that pursuit of interdisciplinarity for its own sake runs the risk of 'adjacent dilettantism' when the parties involved have an inadequate grounding in the characteristic methods and findings of single disciplines. Some early joint teaching ventures were probably more stimulating to teachers than to students for this reason.

Some vital common needs of a more or less utilitarian kind, notably those centring on numeracy, quantitative methods and statistics, could readily be accommodated as School courses; there were also interesting by-products of having to combine indigenous and 'imported' expertise (that of mathematicians) to meet the needs of, say, both economists and social psychologists. Moreover, since the social sciences have always been concerned with, if not defined by, what are loosely called policy issues, where the aim is to assess solutions to contemporary social and economic problems, there was considerable scope for problem-oriented courses which drew on the findings and methods of more than one discipline. The original set of Contextuals contained one cross-School Contextual, *Contemporary Britain*, a course involving a combination of literary and social analysis which was designed to be taken jointly by students in Social and English and American Studies. The formula sustained interest for a few years, but the original set of literary texts bearing on contemporary society became dated, and the focus on Britain alone began to seem unduly parochial for a School that was not defined in geographical or cultural terms. The replacement, *Issues in Contemporary Society*, may have lost its literary component, but it still provides a straightforward way of achieving one of the original goals by offering a wide range of options dealing with the evolving agenda of public debate on such problems as race relations, civil rights, the energy crisis, technological change, and multinational companies which are not the exclusive domain of any single social science, and where members of faculty are able to teach topics that are closely related to their current research.

An equally eclectic policy has been pursued with regard to optional Contextual courses, where we have made use of available expertise in interdisciplinary teams to mount courses which introduce an international dimension (*International Political and Economic Relations*), consider cross-cultural phenomena (*Social Stratification, The World That Others See, Gender Divisions*), respond to student initiatives (*Social Movements and Political Action*), and deal with the cross-disciplinary implications of new approaches (*Social Science of Conflict*) and technological developments (*Computer Models of Mind*). The last of these courses illustrates one of the ways in which the presence of the Cognitive Studies programme in the School since 1974 has contributed to the education of social scientists, though it is, of course, only one example of the much wider and rapid trend towards the use of computers in our teaching and research.

Philosophy originally occupied a more prominent place in the Contextual array of all Arts Schools as a compulsory course: and while a wide range of philosophy options is still available, the contribution of philosophy to the curriculum of the School of Social Sciences is still best illustrated by *Concepts, Methods, and Values* (CMV), the compulsory course taken by all students in their final year. In many ways this has proved to be the most durable of the original courses, though it has evolved along quite different lines from those envisaged in *The Idea of a New University*. The course now consists of two streams, one concerned with the historical development of the social sciences from the Enlightenment to the beginnings of modern professionalisation; the other devoted to a study of those features of the social scientific landscape which are most amenable to philosophical or methodological analysis. History and Philosophy, therefore, while no longer so prominent in other parts of the curriculum, continue to provide valuable second-order standpoints from which to view common problems. CMV has also enabled us to bridge another significant gap, namely that between the social and natural sciences, and to do so in a less contrived fashion than many of the earlier Arts/Science courses, which were based on the simple two-culture view of knowledge prevalent in the 1960s. In this way the course illuminates the elements of a third culture which have been present in the social sciences since their inception, as illustrated by the ambitious attempts of early social theorists to create Newtonian sciences of man in society; and as carried on in the formative mutual relationship between social inquiry and biology before and after the Darwinian revolution. An examination of those respects in which the social sciences are, and yet are not, akin to the natural sciences still provides a major theme in the course. Adapting Kant's description of the chemistry of his day, 'eine Wissenschaft, aber nicht Wissenschaft', we are concerned with the way in which sciences are not Science, and may not ever be. Sussex was founded at what can now be seen as the height of the positivist vogue in the social sciences, and has been able to observe its steady decline from a position that was usually one pace before or behind the general movement, depending on initial tastes.

The success of CMV has not so much been a case of philosophers or historians attempting to legislate a future or a past for the social sciences, but of methodologically or historically-minded social scientists making use of the course to tackle major themes which have never respected the departmental borderlines and hence tend not to be confronted adequately within departmental settings. Since a methodological issue currently troubling geographers or international relations students may have been rehearsed more fully at an earlier stage by economists or sociologists, the history and philosophy of social scientific inquiry acts as a genuine point of comparison and interchange. CMV also provides a forum within which the knowledge claims of fashionable theories and methodologies can be assessed – an invaluable function in disciplines that have been prone to fashion in such matters. The success of the course can partly be judged by the fact that the formula has been copied by other Schools, and partly by the fact that it is now preceded by a first-year course on the *Foundations of the Social Sciences* (FSS) which aims to introduce students at an earlier stage to the issues raised by a detailed study of a limited number of classic texts.

At this point it is necessary to go beyond the confines of the School of Social Sciences. For while this School accounts for half of the students graduating with social science degrees, much that is distinctive about these disciplines at Sussex can be found in the teaching and research done by social scientists in other area-based Schools, and in the relationships which have been established with history and the humanities. An obvious case is provided by African and Asian Studies where those anthropologists, cross-cultural psychologists, geographers, political scientists and economists whose primary concern is with the Third World have created an intellectual environment which supports their interests and matches that to be found in much larger institutions like the School of Oriental and African Studies at London. The Contextual courses on *Comparative Epistemologies*, *Agrarian Societies*, and *Imperialism and Nationalism* entail major contributions by social scientists. A similar, though smaller concentration of social scientists exists within European Studies, where the main concern of economists and political scientists, for example, has been with the problems of the EEC countries and Eastern Europe; and where courses on *Mass Society in Europe* and *Politics, Planning and Society since 1945* make their expertise available to a wider audience.

As far as sociology is concerned, a close relationship with the humanities has been developed which large reflects the theoretical and, at its inception at least, uncharacteristically European orientation given to the subject from the outset. Within European Studies, for example, the connections with European social thought and literary/cultural criticism have been fully exploited. Something similar has occurred in English and American and Cultural and Community Studies, where it is possible for students to choose a combination of courses involving sociology and cultural history. CCS has traditionally been the home of the developmental psychologists, chiefly because the School was originally closely connected with education studies, and one of their main contributions to the School has been the successful cross-cultural course devoted to *Images of Childhood*. CCS is also the home of the more practical side of social studies, namely social work and administration; and it has in recent years become the base from which a multidisciplinary Major in Urban Studies operates, drawing on the expertise of different social sciences to deal with modern urban developments.

In English and American Studies, despite the small numbers of social scientists attached to that School, a degree course in social studies that focuses on America and unites history with politics and sociology has been established which has no real equivalent elsewhere, even in North America. Social scientists have also been fully involved in the School's Contextual courses, mounting options focusing on race and civil rights, and on law and politics. Another contribution has been in the interaction between social theory and literature, where perspectives associated with the social sciences – notably Marxism, structuralism and psychoanalysis – are increasingly being applied to the study of literature and such media as the cinema, calling into question the autonomy of more traditional forms of literary scholarship and critical discourse. Such efforts to disband/expand the borders of cultural analysis open up congenial territory to social scientists, which could explain their contribution to the emergence of a confident post-structuralist strand within the study of Anglo-American and other literature at Sussex.

All of this illustrates a durable feature of the Sussex system of cross-School Majors, namely that it provides scope for multiple centres of experiment and innovation. Each School imparts a distinctive intellectual ethos to the groups it houses, and there would appear to be more variations in the nature of the social science degrees on offer than our size as a university, and the modest number of members of faculty attached to some of our individual groupings, might suggest. Each of these groups has made its own adjustment to the opportunities presented by the system. Thus Economics and Sociology, at one end of the spectrum, have aimed to provide a fairly comprehensive coverage of all their major fields, while Politics has been able to call on philosophers to provide courses on political theory that would be taught within Politics departments at other universities, thereby enabling it to concentrate on public policy issues and the Third World. But all of our degrees depend on the teaching input of neighbouring groups to a far greater extent than is true elsewhere, and I think we can fairly claim that the programmatics of the 1960s have become a reality, and that the degree structure, as improved by experience, has proved robust. At its best, the results fully justify the extra complications which the system introduces into our deliberations; and while, in common with most systems, it functions more smoothly under expansive conditions, it has so far proved flexible in static or declining circumstances, enabling us to switch resources between Contextual and Major subject commitments to ensure a large degree of equity in the sharing of increased burdens.

Undergraduate education in the social sciences gives students a grounding in their Major subject which places them on a par with the best of their peers at other places. The combination of Major and Contextual courses serves those wider vocational ends summarised under the heading of 'transferable skills', namely a knowledge of underlying intellectual principles that are capable of being applied outside their original point of encounter, an ability to analyse complex issues involving both facts and values, and the capacity to draw on disparate sources of information to solve practical problems. To this most tutors would add that Sussex students are likely to possess higher than average abilities as communicators. We can also claim that our arrangements achieve these ends more effectively than traditional Part I/Part II degrees; and that when we do mount Major/Minor combinations, as in the case of Economics with Mathematics or Economic History, the relationships between the two elements have been more fully explored than is often the case with similar negotiated marriages elsewhere.

Over the years we have consistently attracted faculty who have responded to the opportunities presented by ease in crossing, or simply disrespecting, departmental or disciplinary borderlines. There has always been a good deal of role-reversal and interchange, and collaborative teaching and research are still a distinctive feature of everyday life at Sussex, despite the fact that emulation has diluted some of the claims to special status that were common in the early years of the University. Fears that the emphasis on teaching in small groups, with its consequences in terms of heavier teaching loads, would inhibit research have not, on the whole, proved true. Indeed, the freedom to innovate has meant that teaching and research are kept more persistently in close relationship to one another than is frequently the situation elsewhere. Mention has already been made of some of the significant innovations made in recent years and to these can be added the incorporation of Law. This has now been accomplished in a way that adds a promising dimension to the work of social scientists in particular, with the best examples at present being courses on *Legal Thought and Modern Society* and *Human and Civil Rights*. Another important trend can be found in the burgeoning of courses on feminism and gender differences which, taken together, constitute an ambitious women's studies programme.

At the present juncture in the history of British universities, when the social sciences have no good reason to feel that they enjoy official approval, speculation about our future could easily become an exercise in bemoaning stunted opportunities, berating a climate which puts at risk many of those things on which long-term academic distinction depends.* An institution that is still young has little fat, and has become used to making innovations, is bound to feel vulnerable, perhaps even resentful, under what often seem like arbitrarily straitened circumstances. But if we turn what were academic issues during the expansive phase of our fortunes into political or mere trade union ones during the decline, we run the risk of playing somebody else's game. Lack of mobility, with its consequences for our age composition, can lead to insularity and an inability to discriminate between our strengths and

---

* Future historians will find the insistence of the Secretary of State for Education and Science on the elimination of the term 'social science' in the title of the SSRC (now the Economic and Social Research Council) an instructive symbol of government thinking in the 1980s. If Sir Keith Joseph had read a social science degree at Sussex he might have learned that Popper's demarcation criteria are not the last word on the subject.

weaknesses, between what is worth defending and what is more commonplace. Since any changes we may be forced to make must preserve and build on our strengths, it is worth noting those places where our existing base gives access to promising areas for future development.

One of these, undoubtedly, is in the field of Cognitive Studies. Although this is the subject of a separate essay in this volume, it is worth stressing that it began life and remains a programme which has thrived under the roof of the School of Social Sciences as a result of the pioneering efforts of a small group of philosophers and psychologists, joined by linguists and computer scientists, and linked by a common interest in the exciting opportunities presented by computers and the ideas and methods associated with the study of artificial intelligence. The problems of housing such a combination of interests could not have been foreseen in the 1960s, but it is not clear that the enterprise would have thrived so well in any alternative setting. It has also had a desirable by-product in the form of a closer relationship between social and development psychologists, previously divided, and still both separated from experimental psychology by the Arts/Science ravine. Social Psychology is still fairly distinctive to Sussex, with only two or three other universities in the UK having similar concentrations. This enlarged grouping has now extended its research activity from social and developmental psychology to encompass cognitive and clinical psychology.

Social Anthropology has led the way in the application of its characteristic comparative method to European and British sub-cultures, building on its established expertise in dealing with non-European societies. The existence at Sussex of the unique collection of material housed in the *Mass-Observation Archive* provides an opportunity for anthropological and other research on British society that is beginning to be exploited more fully. Anthropologists have also begun to make good use of the links which are now possible as a result of the introduction of Linguistics into the University a few years ago.

Sociology has achieved a broad spread of expertise, ranging from the development of social theory and associated methodological problems to applied social policy and cultural analysis. As with some other groups, its European interests are strong, and it has formed significant alliances outside its borders with students of industrial relations, educational and penal policy, politics and urban studies. An emphasis on public policy questions is, of course, characteristic of many of the social science groupings, especially Politics, Economics and Urban Studies; and here the presence at Sussex of the Science Policy Research Unit (discussed elsewhere in this volume) devoted to the application of social science to policy questions centring on technology and energy is an important resource. The Institute of Development Studies (see the next essay) serves a similar function for Economics, Geography and Politics, all of which have significant concentrations of research interest on the problems of the Third World.

An international as opposed to regional emphasis provides the *raison d'être* for International Relations, where one of the early achievements was the bridge constructed between diplomatic and international history on the one side, and the study of international relations as a network of organisations and systems that were amenable to study from the points of view associated with the social sciences on the other. International economics in the broadest sense is also a major focus of Economics at Sussex, which probably now has one of the strongest collections of specialists in this field in the country, with expertise that extends from matters of fundamental theory to its applications in a policy world characterised by large international organisations of a commercial and inter-governmental nature.

In several respects, the authors of *The Idea of a New University* were more fortunate than their successors today. Their task in surveying solid achievements, as opposed to promising beginnings, was certainly much simpler than it is 25 years later. Any survey of such a broad span of time and territory must entail personal distillation, and I shall close on a more avowedly personal note. We are more 'professional' in our approach than we used to be, and this includes our Contextual courses, some of which were rather hastily assembled in the early days. Growth later required abandonment of what were becoming bottlenecks, but the proliferation of School courses has sometimes produced a *laissez-faire* attitude and a diffusion (sometimes duplication) of effort that makes it more difficult to monitor the nature and quality of that part of the educational experience of our undergraduates which derives from such courses, especially when we make considerable use of extended essays as a mode of final assessment. Diffusion can also mean that members of faculty do not obtain the kind of collective support from colleagues that is important at some stage in everybody's career.

One of the most difficult balances to strike in the social sciences is that between theory and its applications. Such courses as *Concepts, Methods and Values* and *Foundations of the Social Sciences* enable us to confront controversial issues concerning the nature and identity of social theorising, a self-conscious activity which differentiates the social sciences from the other two cultures. The role played by theory is often controversial only in the sense that it is quite illegitimately treated as a term of opprobrium, as 'mere' theory when compared either with the well-established explanatory and predictive structures of *some* natural sciences, or, more usually, with the certainties of blunt common sense and everyday observation. It is true that theory connotes different things to different social sciences, where only economics and some branches of psychology perhaps aspire to construct theories which are both comprehensive and sufficiently closely specified to be capable of being subjected to sustained empirical testing. But the significance of theory in a wider sense goes well beyond the taxonomic and explanatory function which it performs in any systematic inquiry. Among the many things that differentiate human from animal behaviour, let alone from the events and objects of the natural world, is our dependence upon ideas to give meaning to our actions and existence; our capacity, even need, to employ theories as a basis for even the simplest of cultural transactions. It is therefore an essential part of the education of the social scientist to become self-conscious about the belief systems, ideologies and concepts embedded in everyday life in their own as well as other cultures as a preparation for the equally complex task of understanding how the workings of modern societies, economies and polities can be assessed.

92

The critical, philosophical and historical bias of some of our courses is counterbalanced by the way in which research on applied social science and policy questions is rapidly fed into others. Nobody can doubt that the techniques of applied research have become essential to modern societies, though it is less easy to speak of cumulative progress in matters which are liable to be strongly influenced by shifts in the political climate as well as by the welcome recalcitrance of human behaviour. Nevertheless, one of the incidental dangers inherent in the present emphasis on vocational relevance, as with the student pressures towards political relevance prevalent in the late 1960s, is a kind of client mentality, an anxious responsiveness to the actual or presumed priorities of external interests. In the social sciences, as American experience reveals most clearly, the result is usually over-selling followed by disillusionment on the rebound. Those of us who still retain the privilege of teaching the social sciences at Sussex will, therefore, as in the past, have to stand by a calling that avoids over-responsiveness to external interests. I can think of no better way of doing this than to cultivate, in due measure, those more fundamental issues which are nobody's business, if not our own.

7

Sussex and the Third World

Anthony Low

At the beginning of the nineteenth century 20 per cent of the world's population lived in Western Europe. At the beginning of the twenty-first century something close on 5 per cent will. It is remarkable how unnoticed such a large current change continues to be. The peoples of the West continue to think that since they were once at the centre of the world's most dynamic developments, they continue, and will continue to be so. We are thus nonplussed when developments in the Japanese economy dramatically outmarch our own. We find it impossible to believe that South-East Asia has for a long while now been the fastest growing part of the world economically (and, as the traffic on its air routes testify, is at least as dynamically interactive in its development as Western Europe). We are then dismayed by the religious turmoil in the Middle East (with its bruising offshoots in aircraft hijacking). We find it difficult to comprehend that Latin America is fast moving to be the world's major Catholic continent. We are angry when Africa's embattled politicians will not cure their countries' famines and halt their own brutalities. We are bewildered that Britain nowadays counts (beyond a certain nostalgia) for so little in India. And so on.

There is clearly here a huge task to be done in awakening our society to what in other contexts are bluntly called 'the facts of life' – the principal ones being in this connection that we of the West are the human minority, and a shrinking minority at that, and that ordinarily we have a quite inadequate comprehension of what moves those who make up the majority.

It is worth recalling that the study of other cultures and other societies has long played a major role in British scholarship and education. Indeed, for a protracted period these were to an extraordinary extent focused upon the study of Greece and Rome – their languages, their philosophies, their literatures, their history, their drama. The heritage of these studies was then built into the very chemistry of British élite life and thought in a way that no other was – unless it be, in some different respects, the historically contemporary heritage of the Jews. Those influences indicate that there is nothing inherently unconscionable in the endeavours of a latter-day generation to build into a novel concoction of élite British life and thought some understanding of those other cultures and societies that will impinge so increasingly upon it – the mores and methods of that collectivity we dismissively dub the Third World – even if the task calls for some fortitude.

This enterprise has to struggle to find its *forte*. There is, in the first place, the aversion to it born of irritated incomprehension of 'lesser breeds without the law'. To be safe, scholarship and education are still widely felt to need confining to the tangibilities of science and the proximities of western experience. A deal of adventurousness is thus required of those who would venture beyond the confines of Europe and North America in the search for wider human understanding. The task is made none the easier because of earlier ventures down a partial blind alley. Those who first aspired as scholars to explore the worlds east of Suez inevitably (for had they not been brought up in it?) took their models from the well-established classical studies of Greece and Rome. They set to work to immerse themselves in the classical languages of Asia (such as Arabic, Sanskrit, Mandarin Chinese); in their classical texts; and in the extensive religious and philosophic *dicta* expounded there. But there was a vital distinction here. For whereas, so far as western culture was concerned, there were still (despite the discontinuities that could be marked) crucial continuities between the heritage of Greece and Rome and the outlook of, at least nineteenth-century British culture, there was nothing so directly relevant for the British élite in the allegedly comparable oriental classicism; while the arcane obscurities that oriental classicism exposed were, so often, either intensely obfuscating, or well-nigh irrelevant to those Europeans who actually had contact with the East. (It proved indeed, on later investigation, that their critical impressions were often well warranted. Caste in India, for example, bore no more than a problematic relation to the idealist structure that Hinduism's classical texts gave to it.) As for Africa, there was simply a large vacuum (gracefully symbolised by the elephants that overlaid the palpable ignorances of earlier generations of western geographers).

As these disabilities came to be appreciated, so the Orientalists hesitantly extended their remit to enlarge significantly the teaching and study of modern Asian and African languages. This change was symbolised in Britain by the Scarborough Report on Oriental, Slavonic, East European and African Studies, published in 1947. Had the University of Sussex been founded at that time its initial orientations to the Third World could well have been conditioned by that change. In the upshot, however, they waited upon another, and much larger change. That came more generally to be marked by the publication of the subsequent Hayter Report on Oriental, Slavonic, East European and African languages in 1961; though it should perhaps be emphasised that Sussex's plans owed nothing to the Report itself, while owing a very great deal to the change in outlook which it exemplified. This gave novel encouragement to the substantially enlarged employment of the social sciences as the means to greater understanding of Africa and Asia, and signalled a major break with the formerly pervasive orientalist tradition.

There had, of course, meanwhile been a very much larger development that stemmed in the first instance from the vast extension of British dominion over the non-European world. That dominion, it may be stressed, was rarely intensive. Its architects, moreover, were never very numerous (as soldiers and sailors they were more heavily drawn from the generality of Britain's population than is ordinarily understood). To the greater part that stayed at home their adventurings were essentially exotic. But they nevertheless generated a powerful ingredient that became near central to the British psyche. Seen through this prism, this small island stood forth as a great power, for nearly two centuries as the world's greatest power of all. So, Drake, Wolfe, Captain Cook, Livingstone, Gordon and Rhodes each stood larger than life in the national pantheon. 'Rule Britannia', 'red on the map' and 'the empire on which the sun never set', each became powerful ingredients in the national ethos.

In 1947, the year of the Scarborough Report, all this, with India's independence, started to crumble. A decade later Malaya and Ghana had become independent too, and by the time the University of Sussex came into being in 1961, not only had virtually all of Asia become independent, but half of Africa too.

Sussex's involvement with the Third World thus arose quite precisely in the years in which the academically post-orientalist and politically post-imperialist eras began, and from the start has been marked by those particular circumstances surrounding its birth.

The initial idea was that the University should have a School of International Studies, with Martin Wight, Reader in International Relations at the London School of Economics, and *inter alia* author of a history of the Gold Coast Legislative Council, as its Dean. But Wight became head of the School of European Studies instead, and a separate School of African and Asian Studies was then established. Its form was essentially shaped by Asa Briggs and myself on a memorable train journey between Aligarh and Delhi in January 1961. Three years later, in October 1964, it opened its doors. This was no new Haileybury,* nor some new Colonial Service course of the kind Oxford, Cambridge and London had mounted during the post-Second World War years. Certainly, it was to provide for those who wished to serve overseas in Africa or Asia, but its chief educational task was to enlarge the number of those in our society who would be sufficiently knowledgeable about African and Asian cultures and societies so as not to be mesmerised by their palpable differences from our own. (This has become the more important as the children of ethnic minorities, who are nevertheless firmly British, begin their entry into the universities.)

The principal routes to that end have been multiplex. The

---

* The East India College where Malthus once taught, which between 1809 and 1856 trained officers for Britain's East India Company.

emphasis, if not particularly radical, has in the first place been firmly post-imperial: Asia's and Africa's societies have been studied not as the objects of imperial rule but as independent societies standing in their own right. The emphasis has equally been post-orientalist. Thus there have been no classical studies at Sussex, nor any African or Asian language teaching either (a word on this shortly). Modern history, modern literary and philosophical studies, and the social sciences have each been adduced instead as the principal means for advancing understanding of these other societies and their cultures. From the start Social Anthropology has had a prominent place in the School's work, along with its more urban-focused cousin, Sociology. History, Geography, Economics, Political Science, Social Psychology have all figured prominently, too. From near the outset, opportunity has been provided for study of the often highly illuminating literatures from Africa and Asia in western languages; and there has been some provision too for the study of modern Indian and Islamic philosophies and religions. It is characteristic of the general Sussex style that wherever feasible these have all been studied in an interdisciplinary manner. Since such approaches to Africa and Asia are relatively new, dating in many instances from the immediate post-war period, and thus to begin with having very few scholars working in them (it is worth recalling that as late as the early 1950s very few British economists ever ventured upon a study of an Asian or African economy), interdisciplinary cooperation has been their lifeblood. The flow from that into teaching, especially interdisciplinary undergraduate teaching, has accordingly been relatively easy, and, despite a few passing grumbles from those anxious for their own disciplinary credentials, has generally been readily pursued. The overarching coherence of African and Asian Studies as Sussex has pursued them has thus been clear from the start, and that has greatly helped the School – always relatively small by wider Sussex standards – to preserve its strong academic and social *esprit de corps.*

All of this was helped too – though with consequences to which we shall come – by the inevitably somewhat arbitrary concentration on Africa and South Asia. The reasons for that choice in the early 1960s were paradoxical. Africa was an all but certain choice. Britain's media at that stage were full to the brim with Africa. 1960, when more than half the continent had become independent, had been Africa Year, and with the long-running Rhodesian crisis only just opening Africa was still very much on the British conscience. But it was no less important that opportunities for some younger British academics to learn their trade had opened up in the new African universities in the 1950s, so that when Sussex started numbers of these, now with both some teaching and some research experience in Africa under their belts, were available for appointment.

South Asia by contrast had since 1947 been a much neglected place in Britain academically (and in other ways too). In view of Britain's even longer association with it, it seemed high time in 1961 to reverse this. Fortunately, there were just enough of those who had moved into South Asian studies as a consequence of war service in India – two of the School's Professors of Social Anthropology, Freddie Bailey and David Pocock, amongst them – to make this renewed commitment feasible. They were joined by Michael Lipton who had worked on the great Swedish economist, Gunnar Myrdal's, South Asian research project, and by three Australians (coming from the largest source at that time in the western world outside the United States of new South Asian scholars).

The choice of Africa and South Asia as the main foci of the School's attention not only gave the School its range from the start but, by being limited to those two areas, avoided the dangers of too thin a spread. They continue to provide a core sufficiency of contrasts and comparisons to underpin the School's teaching role, as well as securing a pair of research fields within which researchers with adjacent interests can go to work in intellectual association with each other. From the outset the School's first two Professors, Bailey and Low, embarked upon postgraduate training in Social Anthropology and African and South Asian History which soon produced a number of distinguished young scholars, now scattered across the world; and from that start the School's research has steadily burgeoned and expanded.

Given the plethora of indigenous languages in Africa and

South Asia – which made particular languages suitable for graduate and undergraduate teaching well-nigh impossible to select – and the extent to which scholarly work in each of them is principally conducted in European languages (chiefly English but in Africa also French), their choice made the more credible the School's lack of language teaching.

Upon this last issue there will always be two minds. To most people some knowledge of an Asian or African language for those concerned with their study would seem to be a *sine qua non*. But selection here for undergraduate teaching purposes from amongst so many languages would not only have been quite arbitrary but soon very wasteful of teaching resources. For if Hausa, why not Wolof? If Swahili, why not Kikuyu? If Hindi, why not Bengali? If Bengali, why not Tamil? If the School had centred its attention upon the Middle or Far East the choice here would have been easier (Arabic, Mandarin Chinese and/or Japanese). Moreover, had the University not made one of its early mistakes (by not introducing Linguistics from the start, a quintessential Sussex inter-School subject if ever there was one), and particularly if the School had recruited Professor Wilfrid Whiteley to its faculty (who, alas, died before this could be done), a route through this thicket might have been found. But at least the Sussex School firmly avoided the counterpart mistake, which is still far too often committed elsewhere, of simply providing alongside concentrated language study, little more than an academically rootless induction into a compendium of aspects of the related culture and society, very largely divorced from any rigorous training in any single discipline. One of its great strengths from the outset has been that it has always required that its studies of Asia and Africa should be anchored in disciplinary study as this is ordinarily taught, without, to begin with, any particular regard to African or Asian material. No doubt an ideal undergraduate programme in African and/or Asian studies will be made up of three years' cumulative language study together with a firmly discipline-based Major with appropriate specialisms. But all the global evidence is that even where the choice of language is relatively straightforward, this circumscribes much too sharply the opportunities for those who wish to keep their language options open, and, so far as Africa and South Asia are concerned, can only be mounted at excessive cost.

Sussex's diet for those taking African and Asian Studies is instead firmly made up of core work in an established academic discipline – History, Social Anthropology, Geography, Economics, Psychology, Religious Studies, Philosophy, English Literature, French Literature, International Relations or Sociology – along with African and/or Asian specialisms in that discipline, together with work in two or more of the highly fruitful areas in this context where the insights of these disciplines illuminatingly interact with each other. All this can encompass 'development studies', but is by no means confined to them. The principal concerns have been to relate the facts, theories and problems of already well-established academic disciplines to the facts and problems of the world outside Europe and America, and so demonstrate that while human societies share common problems, these nevertheless find different manifestations and resolution in different types of societies. Over the years there has been some extension of the School's interests to Israel, Indonesia, Japan and particularly to the Caribbean. One way of expressing its approach is to say that what Modern Greats has been to Greats at Oxford, Sussex's African and Asian Studies is to Oriental Studies elsewhere. It is an offering that in the post-imperial and post-orientalist period in which it has been pursued, has not only successfully carved out a new furrow, but stood the test of time.

Chiefly because it has been seen to meet such newly felt needs the School has regularly attracted more undergraduates than could originally have been expected. During its first decade there were upwards of 50 or so entrants each year. During the 1970s this number doubled to around 100. With some 30 specialist staff, 300 students in such a School is by any world standards a remarkably high ratio, and makes the more unwarranted the dire threat to its existence which recent and impending cuts present. The essential *raison d'être* of its work lies in the belief that as the world shrinks and the white man's predominance within it, so there will need to be more of the best in our society, as the twenty-first century opens, whose antennae have been attuned to the needs and outlook of societies whose traditions do not originate as ours do in Greece and Rome and Palestine.

One vignette may make the whole point. 1975 saw the tenth anniversary of the School's founding. In celebration of that a dozen or so of its former members had dinner together in (of all places one might think) Waigani township in Papua New Guinea in the Southwest Pacific. Each in their way was involved there. They have since, of course, scattered. But almost all of them are around somewhere, with that experience readily added to the others which the School originally gave them. Well-designed trigger actions, one may say, work.

But all this is only the half of it at Sussex. Since 1966 there has been the Institute of Development Studies as well – *at* the University of Sussex if not *of* the University: a limited company, funded not through the University Grants Committee, but by the Overseas Development Administration; a research institute and development training centre, rather than a university school or department; but a principal part of Sussex's involvement with the Third World, and in a first-cousinly relationship with the University's School of African and Asian Studies, and with the University more widely.

Over the years its orientations have changed; but however drastic at least one of these changes has been, the marks of its founders still lie upon it. The chief of these was Sir Andrew Cohen, the creative head of the British Colonial Office's Africa department in the late 1940s; controversial Governor of Uganda in the early 1950s; highly successful British representative on the UN Trusteeship Council in the late 1950s; and the dynamic first Permanent Secretary of the Ministry of Overseas Development in the 1960s. Cohen shared with Malcolm Macdonald and Hugh Foot (Lord Caradon) the unusual belief (it has to be said) that British decolonisation was above all a positive not a negative step. In his Colonial Office days he created the African Affairs department there to monitor developments and study Africa's needs. Whilst in Uganda he established a Community Development College on the hill behind his Government House. At ODM these two threads in his thinking twined together in his early proposal for a Special Institution to study post-colonial development, and train its practitioners.

When Barbara Castle became Labour's first Minister of Overseas Development in 1964, Cohen's advisory committee on this matter, heavily manned from Oxford, pressed for it to go to Oxford. Cohen was sceptical about that: how many such adjuncts were already scattered around in Oxford? Would Oxford really trouble its mind about one more? He knew and respected John Fulton, Sussex's first Vice-Chancellor, and Chairman of the then important Inter-University Council for Higher Education Overseas. I was also known to him having extensively reported his Uganda Governorship for *The Times*. Cohen thus welcomed a rival bid from Sussex (drafted initially by Barry Supple). In this Fulton committed Sussex to giving pride of place to a Special Institution in its midst, in quite emphatic terms, and this was accepted by Barbara Castle (still jaundiced, so Dudley Seers averred, from her undergraduate years, by Oxford's aloofness). So to Sussex, via a Formation Committee, chaired by ODM's principal economist, Dudley Seers, the Institute of Development Studies (as it was eventually named) came in 1966, with its one fixed point, Tommy Gee, as Cohen's long-determined choice to be its Administrative Secretary.

Like all new institutions it had to probe its way forward in developing its style. It recruited much abler people to its staff than Cohen originally contemplated: Michael Lipton, Colin Leys, Len Joy, Richard Jolly, Ronald Dore, Bernard Schaffer, Hans Singer. Paul Streeten moved from ODM to be its second Acting Director, and was followed as first substantive Director by his erstwhile superior, Dudley Seers. Along with the newer and younger recruits that waxed in this company, this was the galaxy that gave IDS the unique international standing in its field which it very soon secured.

Cohen's concerns were always, however, dual. He wanted issues studied in the most intellectually advanced way that was possible (which was soon assured). But he also wanted the ensuing expertise to be diffused. There was never any thought that IDS would offer undergraduate courses. The plan always was that it should train post-experience practitioners. And so there came into being, from the chrysalis of its planning, the notion of the focused, short-term, post-experience, highly concentrated study seminars which IDS luminaries, and reinforcements from elsewhere, would conduct and teach. Over the ensuing years the study seminars soon became a highly polished, meticulously prepared, much sought after, IDS standby, with its alumni scattered throughout the Third World, not only ordinarily deeply appreciative of its offerings, but soon in innumerable positions of importance and influence. There are other such programmes, in Britain, in Western Europe, in the United States, and in developing countries themselves. But the IDS study seminars have become the yardstick for all of them; at the very least as the first amongst equals of their kind.

But if IDS was not to provide undergraduate courses, and if its principal teaching offering was to be its training courses, it was also clear from the outset that its staff would be available to provide postgraduate supervision too – and that this was a principal reason for attaching it to a university. There were some lines to be cleared here, but Fulton's firm assurance held, and IDS quickly became the most prestigious Development Studies graduate school in Britain, and not easily matched elsewhere either.

One later major development came from a convergence of initially separate ideas. There was always some worry that a doctoral degree by large thesis was not by any means necessarily the best preparation for Development Studies' highflying practitioners. There was soon some feeling that some of the abler study seminar Fellows could do with a stiffer and larger programme. And there was shortly some concern that the offerings which the study seminars were generating were being unnecessarily confined to them. Out of all this came the programme for the two-year M.Phil in Development Studies in 1973, which, many believe, provides a better take-off for the top layer of development practitioners both here and overseas than any on offer anywhere.

Quintessentially Development Studies are a matter for debate. For Cohen the essentials were always relatively clear: more social services and education, more agricultural development, more development of new business enterprises, import substitution, and efficient public administration training. He died before the great debates of the 1970s. In part these were inspired by the fortuitous concurrence around the beginning of the decade of a plethora of attempted societal renewals in Asia (the Cultural Revolution in China, and its offshoots in India and Sri Lanka, along with Bangladesh's Liberation and the rightist New Order and New Society in Indonesia and the Philippines) together with the disturbing rash of political débâcles in Africa. In these circumstances radical Maoist collectivisation seemed to many of those involved to be a far preferable alternative (as variously Cuba, Vietnam and Tanzania appeared to be showing) to the emphasis upon economic growth *tout court* which had previously prevailed; while Franck's argument, founded upon Latin American experience, about the development of underdevelopment (the denudation, especially of African countries, at the hand of colonialists and multinational corporations) seemed to have very much wider application too. IDS in the 1970s could be something of a storm centre for these debates – and at least once was in major difficulties with its ODA paymasters for being so.

But it had its own things to say as well. In the 1970s it was principally responsible for two innovations in the development debate, neither of which satisfied the more radically minded, but both of which had much influence elsewhere, not least in the World Bank, and upon its long running President, Macnamara. The first of these was its doctrine of 'Redistribution from Growth', spelled out more particularly in its reports on employment in Colombia, Sri Lanka and Kenya for the International Labour Office. The second came with its promulgation of 'Basic Needs' for the most seriously impoverished. In addition there were such landmarks as Bernard Schaffer's discussion of the need to secure equitable 'access' in bureaucratic procedures, and Michael Lipton's scintillating book *Why Poor People Stay Poor. A Study of Urban Bias in World Development* (1977); controversial it may have been, seminal it certainly was.

Through these years the Institute's father figures were Dudley Seers and Hans Singer. That was a function not just of their age – older than the IDS average though they were – nor just of the personal affection in which they were held. It turned principally on their exemplary combination of dedication to the cause, versatility in its advancement, and clarity

105

of insight into its needs. If there was a larger problem at IDS it lay in what one of its leading economists called 'the imperialism of economics'. The Institute never, of course, encompassed the development spectrum from one end to the other. If it tried its hand at issues of education and health, and even of militarism (and added the Latin American and socialist economies to its range of core studies), it never possessed expertise in the agricultural and veterinary sciences, which were properly one of the other preoccupations of the World Bank (and indeed of other development operations at home and overseas). It was, however, notably more skewed towards the economists' perspectives than Andrew Cohen for one would have thought warranted. That in part was a simple reflection of its ability to recruit and hold more outstanding economists. But it made it the more vulnerable to its left-wing critics than it might perhaps otherwise have been.

The major threat to its very existence came in the event, however, from the right. In 1979–80 Mrs Thatcher's new Conservative government declared war upon Quangos (quasi-non-governmental organisations). IDS, an independent body wholly funded by ODA, seemed pre-eminently a Quango all through. There was now every indication that steadily and shortly it would lose its government funding altogether. This threat called forth a whirlwind campaign in its defence, culminating in a direct approach to the Foreign Secretary, Lord Carrington, by not least the post-*Brandt Report* Edward Heath. In the event it was agreed that Treasury funding of IDS would continue, but for no more than a Director and twelve Fellows (instead of over 25) along with a minimum of support staff. For the rest, IDS would have to make its own way from income from consultancies and contracts.

Such a major shift naturally much preoccupied the Institute as it advanced towards the start of its third decade. In these years it has kept its study seminars and postgraduate programmes going at as high a level as before, and in the event its Fellowship has responded quite superbly to the threatened body blow. They have secured outside earnings at a higher total level than was ever sought. While there are some clear indications of the disadvantages in being thus distracted from teaching and research by the necessity to bring in outside income, a good deal of development experience gained thereby has been unexpectedly fruitful. Yet as of this writing the dangers to the future of IDS have become patent. The Institute's Fellows, individually and collectively, could clearly earn still more, if this were the choice forced upon them. But they would then simply comprise a consultancy service, and their quite invaluable reflective research and innovative teaching and training over a wide field would in very short order go by the board. That prospect may still be averted – but such cannot be guaranteed. And so much the worse would it then be. For not only is IDS's track record second to none in its field, a remarkable achievement for so young an institution; but its splay of thrusts into the problems of development is now so sharp and broad that its demise, or even decline, would represent a travesty of such remaining post-colonial commitments as Britain proclaims to have. Its future well-being, as that of AFRAS too, is going to require a persistent vigilance.

Sussex's orientations to the Third World as its Silver Jubilee approaches are thus principally twofold. Both have been tempered by two decades and more of experience, and are now firmly placed to move into the coming century with their feet on the ground and their minds in good shape. The School of African and Asian Studies is there to ensure that there are some more in our society than would otherwise be available who have some chance of sensing correctly the wider tides in the larger world that exists around us than Father Thames alone ordinarily records. The Institute of Development Studies is there to ensure that if we have anything to offer to those who struggle with the major problems of poverty, disease and deprivation that afflict the largest masses of humanity it will be forthcoming. In the 1960s Sussex lit two new lights for our global road ahead. They beam still.

8

The Heart of Matter: Physical Sciences at Sussex

Colin Eaborn and Ken Smith

Although this volume celebrates the Silver Jubilee of the University of Sussex, and although we have been associated with it for the whole of that period, it was only in October 1962, when the Falmer campus was established, that science students actually entered the University. During the previous year we visited Brighton and Falmer on a regular basis for planning meetings and to give general supervision to the erection and fitting of the first science building on the campus. In the run-up to October 1962, with the building only half-finished and the campus a sea of mud, we may from time to time have doubted the wisdom of embarking on the enterprise of setting up a new university.

The passage of time has, fortunately, stilled those initial doubts, and we can now take (we hope, justifiable) pride in the achievements of the intervening years. What, ultimately, is remarkable about the physical sciences at Sussex is not a radical new approach to the study of physics or chemistry but rather the extent and distinction of our research. How is it that the Schools of Chemistry and Molecular Sciences and Mathematical and Physical Sciences, starting literally from nothing, have been built up in less than a quarter of a century into centres of research excellence which can justly be claimed, and demonstrated by any criterion of financial support, publications or honours, to rival those of any British university? The answer is to be found in the quality of the academic faculty who were attracted to the University at the outset, and that in turn prompts the question: why did they come to Sussex?

There were several reasons contributing to the decisions to join this new venture, but mainly it was the attraction of the unique and challenging opportunity to design and implement physics and chemistry degree courses from scratch. This was not the end of it, however. We, together with Roger Blin-Stoyle, the three founding science professors, were all active researchers, and were determined that there should be research in the physical sciences from the outset and that it should play a major role in the development of science at Sussex. This was in spite of the view sometimes expressed by our advisers that it would be many years before research could be effectively established. We were enthusiastically encouraged in our resolve by John Fulton, the first Vice-Chancellor, by the willingness of the University Grants Committee to finance the cost of building research laboratories, and by the support of the Department of Scientific and Industrial Research (predecessor to the Science and Engineering Research Council). At that time, however, although we believed strongly in the importance of research in its own right as an essential concomitant of teaching, and as vital from the point of view of attracting good teachers and researchers to Sussex in the future, we had no idea that it would turn out to be so successful.

This remarkable research achievement is one that we hoped for in the early days but hardly dared to expect. It has not, however, been at the expense of teaching activities; indeed, quite apart from the general stimulating effect of active research on teaching, in some areas the two activities are closely intertwined. In this essay we devote a significant part to describing the evolution of the various undergraduate courses and then go on to outline some of the current research programmes.

THE SCHOOL OF PHYSICAL SCIENCES

In the early years the University was small and flexible. New faculty appointed each year had a major influence on both undergraduate programmes and the development of research. The pattern of the latter was initially determined by the specific research interests of newly appointed faculty and, although an overall balance had to be maintained, appointments were made primarily on the basis of ability rather than research field. During the initial period of rapid expansion this was possible, and it was only in later years that more attention had to be paid to consolidating the research pattern.

To begin with, all the Science students and faculty belonged to one School of Studies, the School of Physical Sciences, and the faculty appointed were associated with one of the subject groups – Chemistry, Mathematics, Philosophy or Physics. The initial undergraduate programme of the School may be summarised briefly as follows:

(a) Two-term Preliminary courses were developed which emphasised the mathematical language needed to formulate physical theories and developed an understanding of the properties and structure of matter in terms of fundamental atomic concepts. The courses were intended to be sufficiently flexible for the choice of Major subject to be delayed in many cases until the beginning of the third term. The courses were assessed to provide feedback to students but the results did not contribute towards the final degree.

(b) Undergraduate courses were developed on the assumption that each student would gain specialist understanding by studying for about two-thirds of the time a Major discipline (initially Chemistry, Mathematics, Philosophy or Physics) and also take a Minor science or mathematical course to provide a supportive and broadening element. All the students studied the mathematics relevant to their Major subject and they were also expected to take one of the non-scientific courses organised by both Arts and Science to develop an awareness of the role of science in the world outside the University.

(c) Small group tutorials were organised in addition to the lecture courses to supply the learning needs of individual students, to encourage discussion with faculty, and to help develop the understanding and spirit of enquiry which is an essential part of any degree course.

The single Science School, which is described in detail in *The Idea of a New University*, operated effectively for the first few years when the faculty numbers were small, when new courses were being introduced each term and we had only one science building for teaching and research in the three major disciplines. It became clear, however, that the School would become too large to be managed efficiently and the move of the Chemistry faculty into their own building in 1964, and the foundation of the Schools of Biological Sciences and (Engineering and) Applied Sciences in 1965, provided the opportunity to form the School of Molecular Sciences for the Chemistry-based activities and the School of Mathematical and Physical Sciences for Astronomy, Mathematics, Philosophy and Physics. The name of the former was changed subsequently to the School of Chemistry and Molecular Sciences which, it was thought, would be more attractive to potential students of Chemistry. Although there is still very profitable collaboration and interaction between these two Schools in both research and teaching (for example, in the fields of atomic and molecular interactions and energy studies) they developed quite separately, and we describe these developments in two separate sections.

THE SCHOOL OF CHEMISTRY AND MOLECULAR SCIENCES (MOLS)

At present the following Major subjects are available to chemistry students in the School: Chemistry, Chemistry by Thesis, Chemistry with various Minors (*viz.* Mathematics and Physics, Economics, European Studies, Materials Science, or Polymer Science) and Theoretical Chemistry. The School also offers Majors in Chemical Physics, Environmental Science and Biochemistry. These courses were introduced over the years and have been modified from time to time; some have been available for many years.

For example, the Major in Theoretical Chemistry was introduced alongside Chemistry while the Chemistry Subject Group was still within the School of Physical Sciences and it is still the only degree in this subject in the country. It was created because it was evident in the early 1960s that theoretical chemistry was going to make a major impact on experimental chemistry, and it seemed important that Chemistry students with exceptional mathematical ability should have the opportunity to develop that talent. Entrants are required to show in the Preliminary examination that their mathematical ability approaches that of the best Mathematics students, and they are faced with almost the full Chemistry course and about one-third of the Mathematics course. The numbers are small (typically three each year), but the Major has produced a high proportion of the outstanding scholars emerging from the various Chemistry programmes at Sussex.

The Chemistry by Thesis Major is believed to be unique in Britain (and probably in the world) for any subject. It was introduced in 1970 in response to the criticism that first-degree courses in chemistry (as in other sciences) involve the student in much passive assimilation of knowledge, with little opportunity to display initiative, originality or creativity. In this Major, after the usual Preliminary course, the primary commitment of the student is to a research project. To ensure an adequate general background in chemistry the students are examined on the content of an appropriate selection of the lecture courses in the conventional programmes, but the tests are of a qualifying (pass/fail) nature only, and the level of performance does not count towards the final degree class, which is determined by the quality of the research effort. The programme has operated successfully for 16 years, and has produced several outstanding graduates. None of the serious difficulties predicted by the sceptics when the approach was first proposed has materialised, and the very high standard of the research by the most able students has surprised even the strongest supporters of the scheme. (In several cases the student's work has produced important papers, and examiners have commented that some of the theses would have been acceptable for the D.Phil degree.) The students have the opportunity for personal development which comes from the exercise of initiative and creativity, the need for self-reliance in the management of their programmes, the maturing influence of working alongside postgraduates and post-doctoral Fellows and in close collaboration with members of faculty, and the improvement in the clarity of their spoken and written English which stems from presenting oral and written reports on their researches. The number of students on the course is small, averaging about five per year; this is probably because

1 An aerial view of the Falmer site before the University was built.

2 The same view now.

3   The first Chancellor, Lord Monckton of Brenchley, in the courtyard of Falmer House on the day of his installation (11 June 1963) with (*L to R*) Sydney Caffyn (later Sir Sydney—first Chairman of Council 1959–76); John Fulton (now Lord Fulton, first Vice-Chancellor); Harold Macmillan (now Viscount Stockton), and Paul-Henri Spaak (Secretary-General of NATO), who both received honorary doctorates at the installation; Lord Monckton; Lord Shawcross (first chairman of the Buildings Committee and second Chancellor of the University 1965–85).

4   The first graduation ceremony, 30 June 1964

5   A Students' Union meeting in Falmer House in the mid-1960s.

6   A history seminar in 1985.

7 The Queen's visit to open the library on 13 November 1964.

8   Fred Bayley and Mike Owen in the thermo-fluid mechanics

9 John Maynard Smith delivering a biology lecture.

10 Research students in the Van de Graaf accelerator laboratory.

11 The Gardner Centre art gallery.

12 The computing centre control room.

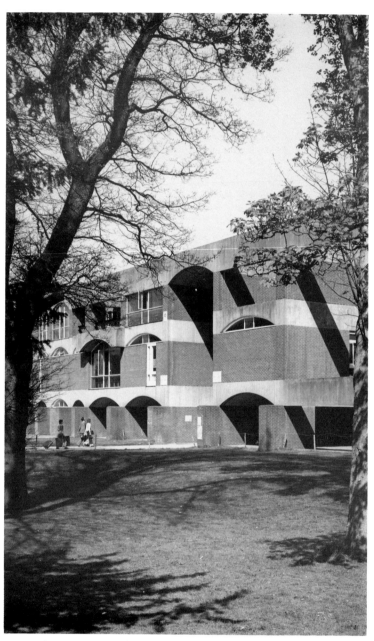

13 Falmer House today.

the availability of this unique course cannot be kept in front of potential recruits in schools. From our experience it seems likely that a significant proportion of students who enter conventional chemistry courses throughout the country would be better served by this Major.

The same can be said of another unusual Major, Chemistry with European Studies, which was introduced into the School in 1978. Entrants must have a basic knowledge of French or German (e.g. a B grade at O-level). In the first year, in addition to taking the usual science courses, they study the relevant language in the Language Centre. In the second year they follow most of the Chemistry course, receive tuition in chemical French or German, and take courses on the *European Economy*, *Science and Technology in the Modern Industrial State*, and *French or German Society*. The third year is spent at a selected university abroad (Bochum, Freiburg, Caen, Nantes or Paris-Sud (Orsay)); reports in the foreign language on this work contribute substantially towards the final degree assessment. The fourth year is spent at Sussex on the course normally followed by third-year students, leading up to the final examinations. There are at present about ten entrants each year to the course, but in view of the special opportunities it offers for personal development and enhancement of career prospects it should surely be taken by many more Chemistry students with the necessary aptitude for languages.

A Major in Environmental Science was introduced in the mid-1970s in response to increasing interest in environmental issues, and in the knowledge that the interdisciplinary spirit at Sussex would provide a favourable climate for it. The programme aims at producing graduates able to set about solving environmental problems, not just to report on them, and thus it involves a substantial part of the Chemistry course along with courses given by faculty from Biology, Geography, Operational Research and the Science Policy Research Unit. There are about ten graduates each year; they are very employable, and take up a wide range of interesting careers. Some of them proceed to postgraduate research in environmental science or chemistry.

The Chemical Physics Major was introduced in 1966,

before the importance of this subject for new high-technology industries, such as those based on optoelectronics, laser technology, optic fibres and integrated circuit devices, had been generally recognised, and the early graduates were thus in an excellent position to contribute to the initial upsurge of activities in those areas. The Major combines the theoretical rigour of the physicist with the pragmatism and broad knowledge of molecular properties of the chemist, and the number of entrants is growing as the importance of the subject is more widely appreciated.

Chemical Physics is also the subject of a one-year MSc course, and there are corresponding courses in Organometallic Chemistry and Medicinal Chemistry; all three arose from the strength of research in these areas in the School, but scientists from the Wellcome Research Laboratories make a major contribution to the teaching of Medicinal Chemistry. An MSc course in Energy Studies is offered in collaboration with other Schools. The great majority of the MSc students come from overseas, and many stay on to work for the D.Phil.

The creation of a new research school in Chemistry from 1962 onwards provided an opportunity to concentrate on areas of the subject which seemed likely to be of increasing importance for the rest of the century. Those selected were theoretical chemistry, biological chemistry, physical organic chemistry, organometallic chemistry (with related aspects of inorganic chemistry), chemical physics and polymer chemistry. This choice has proved to be sound, and has not only enabled Sussex to become internationally recognised as a centre of excellence for chemical research, but has also provided a firm basis for advance in the future. The unusually high level of research collaboration in the School between workers within the same field and between groups in different fields has contributed greatly to the overall success.

At present there are 31 full-time members of faculty in the School, 30 post-doctoral Fellows, 120 research students (a good number on SERC CASE awards involving joint research with industrial organisations), and 23 MSc students. In the period January 1980 to July 1985 some 850 papers and 12 books were published. Associated with the School at present are a Nobel Laureate (Sir John Cornforth), five Fellows of the

Royal Society, a SERC Senior Fellow (Professor Michael Lappert), and winners of many senior awards of the Royal Society, the Royal Society of Chemistry and the American Chemical Society. (At one time, when Professor Archer Martin (Nobel Laureate) and (the late) Professor Alan Johnson were present, there were seven Fellows of the Royal Society.) Sir Ronald Mason was the Chief Scientist at the Ministry of Defence in 1979–83. In 1981 Professor Joseph Chatt received the ($100,000) Wolf Prize for Chemistry, ranked second only to a Nobel Prize, and is the only British chemist to have done so. The success of the research has also been recognised by the high level of research income from non-UGC sources; for example, Sussex was ranked fourth in the country in 1982–84 in terms of the value of research grants awarded by the SERC Chemistry Committee.

In the space available only a fraction of the research in the School can be mentioned, and in the examples below the emphasis is on projects which have obvious potential applications. It must be appreciated, however, that these are not necessarily the most important, since it is the fundamental advances today which will provide the basis for applications in the future.

In biological (including medicinal) chemistry Frank McCapra has had striking success in elucidating the mechanism of bioluminescence, the chemical process involving the enzyme luciferase whereby living creatures such as fireflies, glow worms, some deep sea animals and certain bacteria produce light. His work has led to the development of 'cold light' devices for emergency lighting, and the chemiluminescence of some of the compounds synthesised during the work has been shown to be very sensitive to the presence of species such as hormones and drugs, which opens the way to construction of 'biosensors' to monitor such substances in biological fluids; this approach could well replace the somewhat hazardous radioimmunoassays currently used. Studies by Douglas Young of molecular processes central to cancer chemotherapy have provided much insight into the action of the anti-leukaemic drug methotrexate. He has also produced novel penicillin-related antibiotics designed to have increased potency, and is elucidating the molecular processes involved in blood clotting.

115

Work with even more direct medical implications is being carried out by Malcolm Topping, who, in an imaginative application of the methods of the physical organic chemist to a physiological phenomenon, has defined a new type of blood classification based on the inhibitory response of human α-2-macroglobulin to attack by proteolytic enzymes, seven different types of response being distinguishable. The work, performed in cooperation with leading hospitals, has shown that the distributions of the responses over a group of patients suffering from various diseases, such as emphysema, asbestosis, liver disease, diabetes, cancer and rheumatoid diseases, differ from one group to another, and all of them from that for healthy people; the approach has much potential as an aid to diagnosis, and should lead in the long term to important advances in the understanding of the diseases and so in their treatment. One important observation is that physiological changes are produced in a group of people (not necessarily in any individual) by exposure to asbestos dust at levels far below those usually regarded as dangerous, and many years before clinical symptoms of disease could be expected. Jim Hanson is mainly studying steroids and terpenoids from plants and fungi, and he has produced a novel group of plant growth regulators which may find application in agriculture.

The School has for many years been internationally recognised as a centre of excellence for organometallic chemistry (concerned with compounds containing metal–carbon bonds), a field of considerable importance to industry. The first representatives of many classes of interesting compounds were made at Sussex (largely by Michael Lappert's group), especially those having the metals in unusual oxidation states, coordination numbers and bonding modes. The fact that Sussex is a world leader in organosilicon chemistry prompted Dow Corning plc (a subsidiary of the Dow Corning Corporation, the world's largest silicones company) to establish its European Research Group in the School's laboratories.

A major stimulus to the work in organometallic and transition metal chemistry in the School has come from the presence under the same roof of the AFRC Unit of Nitrogen Fixation. The aim of the Unit is to determine the mechanism of the process whereby certain microorganisms, including some which infect the roots of leguminous plants such as clover and beans, can transform nitrogen into ammonia, a conversion which in the chemical industry requires temperatures of several hundred degrees and pressures of several hundred atmospheres. The Unit, which is unique in the breadth of expertise and the disciplines brought to bear on the problem, has made considerable progress towards its important objective.

In the field of chemical physics, Harry Kroto's identification of molecules in interstellar space has attracted the widest attention, partly because of its possible relevance to the problem of the origins of life. After the synthesis at Sussex of types of compounds he suspects may be present in outer space, he determines their spectra then goes to a radiotelescope in North America to look for appropriate frequencies in space. In this way he detected the largest interstellar molecule so far reliably identified, following the synthesis of related species by David Walton's group.

The polymer science group is concerned with production of new tailor-made polymers, including liquid crystal polymers, and with the mechanisms of formation and degradation of polymers. In an advance which is attracting considerable industrial interest, Norman Billingham has devised an inexpensive method of measuring weak light emitted by plastics (and other organic materials) when they undergo oxidation, and thus of determining the rate and extent of their degradation.

As a final example of the very varied research carried out in chemistry-related fields, it should be noted that the School was for some years the largest producer of iron and steel in the county of Sussex, the output averaging several grams per day! The work was initiated by Ivor Nixon, a very distinguished chemical engineer and inventor who had been head of the Shell refinery operations worldwide and also of the technological economics division of the company. (His name is familiar to nuclear engineers through the 'Nixon kilns' he devised to make the pure graphite needed as the moderator for the first nuclear reactors, and has long been known to students of chemistry through the Mills–Nixon effect, which was based on research he carried out in the 1920s as an undergraduate at

Cambridge). His work at Sussex resulted in many patents for the Sussex Direct Reduction Process, the Sussex Steel Process, and the Sussex Integrated Steel process, and it is likely that when the severe recession in the steel industry is over, the processes (or at least aspects of them) will be put into operation. David Smith, who cooperated with Ivor Nixon on some of the work, is continuing research on direct reduction.

A few years ago there was concern in the School about the age distribution of the academic faculty (a national problem), which held the prospect that there would soon be no member of faculty in the School under about 45 and very few under 50 years old, with a threat of a decline in enthusiasm for research. There has been no sign of such decline, and research in the School in recent years has probably been at its most effective ever, but even the hypothetical threat has been removed by the appointment in the last three years of four young Lecturers (one under the SERC Special Replacement Scheme and three under the New Blood Scheme), a (five-year) SERC Research Fellow and a (five-year) Royal Society University Research Fellow. With the youthful enthusiasm of these very able young people complementing the continuing liveliness of the highly productive established groups the research future of the School seems assured.

THE SCHOOL OF MATHEMATICAL AND PHYSICAL SCIENCES (MAPS)

The School of Mathematical and Physical Sciences, grew rapidly to become the largest of the Science Schools. Three connected buildings now provide the office, teaching and research space for the 65 faculty appointed to the Subject Groups (Astronomy (4), Logic and Scientific Method (3), Mathematics (28), and Physics (30)) as well as approximately 20 Research Fellows, 10 visitors, 60 postgraduate students and 360 undergraduates.

The majority of the faculty appointed to teach physics in MAPS took up their posts during the first four years of the University's existence. They practise what has been argued by many to be the parent science because it deals at a fundamental level with the widest range of concepts in both space and time, and which, it is argued, should therefore occupy a dominant position in the scientific world. University-level physics attracts many able students, influenced, perhaps, by the intellectually challenging nature of the discipline and by the fact that physicists have readily found employment in industry and research establishments as members of multidisciplinary teams and also as administrators.

Astronomy was introduced into the University in 1965–66 when Bill McCrea (now Sir William) set up the Astronomy Centre financed by the Science Research Council, and Roger Tayler was appointed to the Chair of Astronomy. The decision to teach astronomy was taken because of the proximity of the Royal Greenwich Observatory (RGO) at Herstmonceux and the first teaching, for an MSc course, was given by the staff at the RGO headed by the Astronomer Royal, Sir Richard Woolley, who was appointed a Visiting Professor. Astronomy was, and still is, a predominantly postgraduate subject although from the start some third-year options and projects were made available to Physics majors.

The Major in Philosophy in the School of Physical Sciences was first approved in the academic year 1961–62, a year before Science students arrived. Within a few years the emphasis had moved towards the philosophy of physics and mathematics and the title was changed in 1971 when Jerzy Giedymin came to Sussex from the University of Poznan, Poland, to become Chairman of a reorganised Logic and Scientific Method Subject Group.

The range of Physics courses available has now grown to include a number of Minor courses from other Schools in both Arts (e.g. Economics, European Studies) and Science (e.g. Electronics, Microcomputing). The two-term Preliminary period with School examinations which do not contribute to the final degree has remained, but the emphasis for Physics majors during this period is now more on the initial development of the basic concepts needed for the Major course instead of the *Structure and Properties of Matter*, which was designed originally to introduce important concepts common to physics and chemistry. The second-year Arts–Science courses continue to be taken with enthusiasm by many students although, sadly, the scheme has been abandoned for students on the Arts and Social Studies side of the University. The courses which present the main conceptual ideas of physics as a discipline come in the first two years, together with laboratory work primarily designed to support the lecture courses, but also to enable students to study some of the more important techniques currently associated with experimental physics. In the third year the majority of the Physics courses are chosen from some 30 School options and the students take what is for many the most interesting course of all, a theoretical or experimental two-term project which is often carried out in one of the research laboratories in collaboration with graduate students or a Research Fellow. All Physics majors learn to use a computer to solve physics problems and microprocessors are beginning to play a significant role in the control of classroom experiments and projects.

The Minor courses now available with Physics as a Major subject are Astronomy, Chemistry, Economics, Electronics, European Studies, Mathematics, Microcomputing, Philosophy of Science, Physics and Social Dimensions of Science. There is also a joint course in which the main Mathematics and Physics courses are combined to give an effective introduction to theoretical physics. Students who want to maximise project work and the applications of physics take the Physics Minor together with the Major. The main aim of the Microprocessor Minor is the development of the techniques needed for computer control of experiments and the analysis of data, skills which are important when the students leave to work in industry. The increasingly popular European Studies Minor, the basic aims of which have been discussed at greater length in the section on Chemistry and Molecular Sciences, provides the opportunity to learn to communicate in a European language well enough to work efficiently overseas.

There is little doubt in the minds of faculty, as was stressed at the beginning of this essay, that innovation and competence in teaching are enhanced significantly when the teachers are actively engaged in research work. This is true in physics, where progress with almost any research project in either pure or applied physics is dependent on technological developments which in turn await new discoveries at the frontiers of physical science. Contact with industry is essential, and it is also important that undergraduate courses include some of the recent industrial developments or they soon lose touch with the world outside the University.

Research in physics takes place not only within the University but also at major establishments overseas and it involves the installation of expensive equipment financed by grants from the Science and Engineering Research Council and other bodies. For the last five years the Physics Subject Group has consistently ranked fourth in the allocation of such funds behind only the considerably larger physics departments at Cambridge, Imperial College and Oxford, and the total sum received over the five-year period amounted to £4.8 million. Extensive electron microscope facilities and three accelerators have been installed for the study of the structure and surfaces of solids and the Subject Group has been recognised by SERC as a centre both for research in the field of ultra-low temperatures physics, which involves experimental work close to the absolute zero of temperature, and also for research using the very high magnetic fields produced by superconducting magnets. In addition to this direct support, two groups make extensive use of facilities at the nuclear physics laboratory at Daresbury, England and the Institute Laue Langevin in Grenoble, France. The quality and significance of the research in physics at Sussex has been recognised in the wider physics community by the fact that during the past five years the Subject Group has included three Fellows of the Royal Society, holders of the Rutherford Medal and Prize, the Maxwell Medal and Prize, the Simon Memorial Prize of the Institute of Physics, one SERC Senior Fellowship, three SERC Advanced Fellowships and a Royal Society University Research Fellowship. Some 445 research papers were published by members of the Physics Subject Group during this period. The Subject Group has 20 formal collaborative agreements with other universities throughout the world including one supported financially by the British Council under its Academic Links with China Scheme, which has resulted in the exchange of faculty for teaching and low temperature research with Nanjing University. In previous years similar academic links existed with the University of Kumasi, Ghana and the University of Ife, Nigeria.

There are four broad research groups within which the Physics Subject Group organises its research, its research seminars and its graduate courses. Only a brief mention of some of the research underway can be made here but it should illustrate the very varied interests of Sussex physicists and astronomers.

The solid state and applied physics group uses accelerators and clean surface electron microscopes to study metals, insulators and semi-conductors in order to understand better the behaviour of solids in terms of the interactions between the constituent atoms. The group's work is carried out in close collaboration with industry and includes the study of low-dimensional solids which may be important in the next generation of computer chips, and the way the optical properties of materials are modified by ion bombardment to develop properties suitable for the fibre-optic industry.

The work of the faculty in the low temperature group centres on the study of thermal, magnetic and other properties of materials at temperatures within milli-degrees of absolute zero in order to understand their low temperature behaviour in terms of the interactions between their constituent atoms. At the same time some of the group's work is carried out in collaboration with industry and is aimed at exploiting new cryogenic developments. A newly installed superconducting very high magnetic field system is now in use as a regional facility to study the behaviour of the electrons in ultra-pure metals, alloys and weakly magnetic materials. The development of superconducting devices as ultra-sensitive magnetic field detectors with applications in many sciences including medicine has been extended to a new study of the quantum properties of solids at low temperatures.

The atomic, laser, plasma and nuclear group is interested in experimental nuclear and particle physics and makes extensive use of the high neutron flux nuclear reactor in Grenoble, France and the SERC heavy ion accelerator at Daresbury, England, to measure the lifetime and electromagnetic properties of one of the basic building blocks of matter – the neutron. Other experiments, which involve the use of ultra-low temperatures as well as nuclear instrumentation, are designed to find out more about the structure of nuclei and the nature of the forces between fundamental particles. SERC has also made substantial investments in equipment at Sussex for laser studies of the fundamental interactions between radiation and matter. Some of the plasma experiments set up to study the upper atmosphere involve sophisticated equipment operating in the GEOS and AMPTE satellites, with the results being analysed on a computer installed at Sussex. Very high velocity impact experiments, which are fundamental to an understanding of the development of planetary surfaces (for example, the 'dimples' on the moon) are studied in close collaboration with an Italian group using very fast cameras and plasma probes to record the development of impacts at speeds in excess of 10 km/s produced by explosive techniques.

Research in theoretical physics ranges widely and has often been carried out as close collaboration between theory and experiment. The general theory of systems composed of many closely packed strongly interacting particles is studied in order to understand better the subtle details of the behaviour of, for example, metals and alloys, condensed gases, quantum liquids at very low temperatures and the motion of atoms very near solid surfaces. Research in nuclear theory has resulted in the development and evaluation of new models of the nucleus and a detailed study of the forces acting on fundamental particles inside the nucleus. In elementary particle theory one of the main topics studied has been the breakdown of basic physical laws at the very high energies now available in modern laboratories. There is also a study in collaboration with the Astronomy Centre of the cosmological implications of recent developments in elementary particle theory.

The members of the Astronomy Centre research, in fact, in most branches of theoretical astrophysics and cosmology and a wide variety of observational work is done through collaboration with the RGO. Present observations suggest that the universe started with what is known as the 'Big Bang' about 15,000 million years ago and the key to its whole future development may lie in what happened during the first few minutes after the origin. This is one of the chief research interests of Sussex astronomers. A second major field is the role of magnetic fields in the universe with particular reference to the process of star formation and the properties of highly compact stars known as pulsars. Members of the Centre have published about 250 research articles in the past five years, two are Fellows of the Royal Society, one a gold medallist of the Royal Astronomical Society, and one an SERC Senior Fellow.

The foregoing outline of some of the research interests of physicists and astronomers at Sussex is, of course, extremely sketchy. Some of this research has immediate and direct applications to technology and industry. But a large part of it is concerned with simply attempting to understand the fundamental processes of nature – for example, the way matter behaves at temperatures which do not occur naturally on earth or the way fundamental particles interact with each other at energies which only occurred when the universe was being created. Research of this latter kind generally has no obvious applications. But the same was said in the past of research which is now the basis of present-day technology. It is the job of universities to ensure that research of this kind continues and we certainly intend to do so at Sussex.

We now have well-equipped physics laboratories and a lively, diverse research programme extending from the very applied to the very pure. We are confident that the creativity and productivity of the well-established groups will continue, in spite of the fact that most of the faculty are now over 45 years of age, so long as the youthful enthusiasm so essential for the continuing development in both research and teaching continues to be provided by the appointment of able young faculty like the two who recently joined us under the New Blood Scheme.

9

Integrating the Biological Sciences

John Maynard Smith

The establishment of the new universities in the 1960s came at a fortunate time for biologists. It had been apparent for some time that training in biology, in the universities and to some extent in the schools, was in a mess. In organisation and curricula, British universities still reflected the state of science as it was in the nineteenth century. At that time, the main task of biologists was the description and classification of the vast variety of animals and plants that had been discovered. There was, therefore, a natural division of labour into botanists and zoologists, and within zoology, for example, into entomologists, vertebrate zoologists, and so on. Reflecting this, the main biological departments in British universities were of zoology and botany, and, at least in zoology, the main content of the courses was comparative anatomy.

This state of affairs was not confined to universities that were relatively inactive in research. University College London, at which I took an undergraduate degree in zoology after the war, and at which I taught until I moved to Sussex in 1965, was in the forefront of research in subjects such as genetics, immunology and neurobiology. Yet, right up to 1965, the core of the zoology degree consisted of comparative anatomy. Vertebrates and invertebrates were taught in alternate years, so that it was a matter of chance whether an entering undergraduate spent two years studying the former or the latter. Most of the faculty teaching these courses were not themselves doing research in anatomy, and some of us were rather ignorant of the subject-matter. Yet, during my twelve years as a Lecturer there, I never gave a lecture course in my own disciplines of genetics and evolution, although I was allowed to run a practical class in genetics.

This pattern, which was typical of British universities, was broken by the establishment of the new universities, and in particular by the Schools of Biological Sciences at York and at Sussex. I had been grumbling about the training we had been giving our students at UCL for years, but was powerless to alter it. The chance to start a new kind of training in biology at Sussex was too good to miss, even if it did mean spending a lot of time at first on administration. Fortunately, I was not alone in feeling fed up with the state of biology in the universities, so that it was easy to find others whose outlook was similar to my own. The faculty who joined the School when it opened in 1965, and to a considerable extent those who have arrived since, did so because they were keen to teach an integrated course in biology.

I shall describe the principles upon which we designed our courses, because they are those upon which we still operate. There are, in effect, two ways of planning a university course in biology, which I shall call the integrated and the supermarket methods. On the integrated approach, one attempts to identify the main principles that underlie the subject, and to design a course which will teach those principles. On the supermarket approach, one offers a large number of unit courses, and allows the individual student maximum freedom to put units together to construct a degree. The latter has some obvious advantages: it enables each faculty member to teach the thing he or she really cares about, and it gives a lot of freedom to individual students to pursue their own interests. It has, however, a fatal drawback: it fails to allow for the structure of scientific knowledge. Thus it is often the case that one cannot understand B until one has understood A. To give an example from my own field, one cannot understand the evolution of social behaviour until one knows some population genetics, and one cannot understand population genetics until one knows Mendel's laws. In designing an integrated course, one can take these constraints into account, and make sure that A is taught before B. With the supermarket method, one cannot easily guarantee this. The students taking a unit course will have different backgrounds, so that the course often has to start by going over essential material that is familiar to one half of the students but not the other half. The result is that, with the integrated approach, one can get deeper into the subject by the third year than is possible with the supermarket approach.

We have tried to combine the advantages of the two methods. During the first two years, students following a particular Major (for example, the Biology Major, which accounts for about half the undergraduates in the School) follow a single integrated course, which does attempt to give a picture of biology as a whole. Because it is followed by all students in the Major, later courses can rely on knowledge acquired in earlier ones. Freedom of choice is provided in two ways. First, the third year is run essentially on supermarket principles. A wide range of courses is offered, depending primarily on the research interests of the faculty, and each student is free to choose any four units, subject only to timetable constraints. This means that a student majoring in Biology can spend the third year specialising in, say, genetics and cell biology, or in population biology, or in neurobiology, or can select units from different fields. In each case, the necessary background will have been laid in the first two years.

The second way in which choice is maintained is through the existence of a range of Major subjects. There are seven Majors in the School: these will be described later. Undergraduates enter the School to read a particular Major, but there is a large degree of freedom to switch to another Major during the first two terms. This freedom is not absolute: for example, a student who entered the school to major in Experimental Psychology, and who had done no chemistry at school, could not switch to Biochemistry. Nevertheless, freedom is extensive, and does, in particular, enable students to switch to Majors such as Neurobiology that they probably did not know about when still at school.

We think that, by combining an integrated core course for the first two years with a variety of Majors, and a wide range of third-year options, we get the advantages of the integrated and the supermarket approach. Before discussing how the core course is constituted, I cannot resist commenting on how the established universities responded to the existence of schools of biology in some of the new universities. They could not ignore them, because they were losing too many good applicants, so they too had to offer a degree course in biology. But it is very hard to design an integrated course to be taught by a series of separate departments, whose members have probably been quarrelling for years. The result, understandably, has been that a supermarket approach has been adopted, with each department offering its own courses, and with little attempt to integrate. To make matters worse, biochemistry departments have often felt strong enough to remain outside such schemes, so that many biology degree courses lack any significant biochemical input. Despite my own ignorance (thanks to UCL) of biochemistry, I suspect that this is a mistake. To be fair, some universities (Leicester is an example) have overcome these difficulties, and offer a biology degree course similar to the one offered at Sussex. Even those that have not have been shaken out of the nineteenth-century straitjacket that held them as little as 20 years ago.

It is easy enough to say that one will design a course that will teach the principles of biology, but harder to identify those principles. T. H. Huxley, in the last century, was an eloquent advocate of the educational value of comparative anatomy, whereas I tend to see it as a dead end. As it happens, I think that both opinions are correct. Science does not stand still. The principles that students need to learn are those that are likely to be important during their lifetime. For those trained during the latter part of the last century, comparative anatomy was indeed going to be important for research during their working life: it is much less so today.

It seemed to me in 1965 that there were various topics that were likely to be important in the immediate future, although the reasons were somewhat different in different cases. The first, and obvious, candidate was molecular biology – that hybrid between genetics and biochemistry that dominates so much of biology today. It was not obvious then – and, indeed, is not obvious now – exactly what the consequences (theoretical and practical) would be of the recent discovery of the chemical basis of heredity, but it was clear that the consequences would be important. The next two candidates were, in effect, problems that are at the same time important and unsolved. The first is the problem of how an egg turns into an organism, and the second the problem of how the brain works. There is an obvious danger in identifying unsolved problems, however important, as future areas of research. As Medawar has remarked, science is the art of the possible. Development and brain function will be important research areas only if people find ways of making progress. However, there were reasons for thinking that the time was ripe for making progress in both these fields, and I think that the guess has been justified.

The fourth area was the study of natural populations, both in their ecology and in their evolution. I do not think it is sensible to study ecology and evolution as separate disciplines. In so far as there is a central concept in modern biology, it is that of evolution by natural selection. It is an odd fact that the Biology course at Sussex is one of the rather few in which this central role is recognised.

The core course in Biology, then, was originally planned to equip students to work in four main problem areas – molecular biology, development, brain and behaviour, and ecology and evolution. Of these four areas, only one is peculiar to higher animals: the others are equally relevant to animals and plants, and microorganisms are crucial for the study both of molecular biology, and of ecology and evolution. Hence, although we avoid courses on the anatomy and taxonomy of particular groups of organisms, the curriculum as a whole does inculcate some familiarity with a wide range of kinds of organisms.

The School was originally conceived as a single group of teaching faculty and of undergraduates, but two developments, one planned and one almost accidental, have to some degree altered that. The planned development was in biochemistry. Research in most areas of biology requires some knowledge of biochemistry. All Biology majors do some biochemistry, and some specialise in that field in their third year. However, it seemed right to start also a Biochemistry Major, consisting partly of the biochemistry, genetics and cell biology components of the Biology Major, and partly of additional courses in chemistry and biochemistry. The introduction of this Major carried with it a substantial increase in teaching and research faculty in Biochemistry.

129

The second new Major was unplanned – at least by me. The first Professor of Psychology appointed at Sussex was Stuart Sutherland, who sees psychology more as a science than as an arts subject. The natural home for him and his colleagues was therefore in the School of Biological Sciences, and there is today a very active group of psychologists in the School. The first result was the introduction of a Major in Experimental Psychology. This was followed by a Major in Neurobiology, which is a combination of courses in experimental psychology, and courses in neurophysiology and animal behaviour. This is a unique Major, made possible by the presence in a single building and School of both biologists and psychologists. Since the degree is an unusual one, graduates find it easier than most to find an opening in research.

Another consequence of the presence of Experimental Psychology was the birth of Artificial Intelligence studies at Sussex. This originated with the appointment in the School of Biological Sciences of two Professors in Artificial Intelligence, Christopher Longuet-Higgins (a convert from theoretical chemistry) and Max Clowes. This research has since spread to the School of Engineering and Applied Sciences and to the Arts side of the University.

I have so far mentioned four of the seven Majors – Biology, Biochemistry, Experimental Psychology and Neurobiology. The three others are Geography, Human Sciences and Biology with European Studies. Geography majors spend half their time doing biology courses, mainly those in ecology, evolution and plant physiology and half studying geography, particularly physical geography. The Human Sciences Major is a four-year course, consisting partly of biology, and partly of courses in psychology, anthropology and linguistics taught on the Arts side of the University. It is unusual in having an approximately equal input of arts and science courses. It places a rather heavy demand on students, because of the very different methods and requirements of faculty on the two sides of the University, but I have usually found the students of this Major great fun to teach. Finally, the recently introduced Biology with European Studies Major is also a four-year course, adding a year studying biology in a French or German university to the standard Biology Major.

The School has just completed a review of its undergraduate courses, to see how far, after 20 years, there is a need for revision. The review was carried out in the main by people who have joined us after the original pattern was established. By and large, they have concluded that we got things about right, although perhaps we swung a bit too far away from the descriptive zoology and botany characteristic of the 1960s. The main reform that has been introduced as a result of the review is the introduction of a course in computing. We have equipped a laboratory with micros available for under-graduate use, and are now running a course in programming, and in the use of computers to analyse biological problems.

So far, I have written of the teaching of undergraduates. I now turn to the School as a centre of research. It was in this context that those of us who came to Sussex in the early days took the greatest gamble. It was clear that we could, within reason, develop what teaching courses we liked, but it was less obvious that research would flourish. There was a view abroad that the new universities would do little research, and that Sussex would be a liberal arts college by the sea. As it has turned out, research in biology, as in the other sciences, has flourished.

A few statistics will indicate the scale of our research. There are 42 permanent members of the teaching faculty. During the past five years, members of the School have received £7,000,000 in research grants, from the Research Councils, from foundations and from industry. Over 1000 scientific papers (excluding book reviews and popular articles) and 29 books have been published. In the same five years, 132 students have been awarded D.Phils. The School obtained four New Blood lectureships: since these were allocated in competition with other universities, the fields in which they were awarded indicate the particular subjects in which the School has a high reputation. These fields were in the psychology of hearing and of vision; in molecular genetics applied to development; and in the development of the nervous system.

There is no way in which I can summarise such a wide field of research. Instead, I shall mention a few topics of which I have some personal knowledge (as I do not, for example, in biochemical endocrinology, or in plant physiology, or in cognitive psychology, all of which have been outstandingly successful). I start with my own subject – evolutionary biology. For the past ten years, Sussex has been the main centre in Europe for the study of evolution. Each year we have had a number of visiting scientists, on grants or on sabbatical leave, from countries as far apart as Japan and the US, and from Brazil to Norway. As a result, ideas that originated here are now influential all over the world. One recognition of this is that the most recent meeting of the International Congress of Systematic and Evolutionary Biology, which meets every five years, was held on the campus. I hope that evolutionary studies will continue, although inevitably they will suffer with the departure of Brian Charlesworth to Chicago and Paul Harvey to Oxford.

Next, I shall say something of research in neurophysiology and animal behaviour. Ian Russell was the first to record electrically from the hair cells in the cochlea of the ear. Richard Andrew has demonstrated a differentiation of function between the left and right hemispheres of the brain of the chick. Tom Collett has proposed simple but convincing explanations of how insects, toads and mammals find their way about. Mike Land has discovered new optical processes, involving mirror and waveguide optics, in the eyes of insects and crustacea. This work, which contributed to Land's election to the Royal Society, has led to a new design for an X-ray telescope. This particular story has a moral for the planning of science. No one could possibly have foreseen that work on the eyes of shrimps would lead to engineering applications. Fundamental research does lead to useful applications, but it cannot be planned with these applications in mind.

The third topic I want to discuss also has a moral, this time for how we should teach scientists. From the beginning, we have had an active interest in development, and in the use of genetical techniques in its study. It is perhaps in this field that graduates of the School, now working in other places, have made the greatest impact: I have in mind particularly the work of Vernon French, who was one of our first undergraduate intake in 1965, and of Jonathan Cooke and Peter Bryant, who were two of our first D.Phil students. I think that the reason why some of our ablest students became interested in development was that they were confronted, while here, with two very different views about how research on development should be pursued, from Brian Goodwin and James Sang, who were both founder members of the School. Goodwin (now a Professor at the Open University) takes an obstinately holistic attitude to the problem, whereas Sang (who in theory retired seven years ago, but who is still receiving grants to support his research in the School) has a geneticist's strictly reductionist attitude. Despite their differences, they taught courses together, so that students were forced to think far more deeply about the subject. One cannot easily plan to have students faced by opposing views in this way, but if it happens, and particularly if it happens in a friendly atmosphere, it is certainly stimulating. Although Goodwin has left, and even Sang cannot go on for ever, research on development is still active, and has been strengthened by the two New Blood Lecturers, Jonathan Bacon and Julian Burke.

It is worth asking whether research has benefited by the presence in a single School of psychologists, biologists and biochemists. It is hard to be sure, but I do think that our School structure has been one factor contributing to the success of research. At the simplest level, it makes it very easy to get advice and technical help. I know that I have been helped by colleagues in disciplines as diverse as biochemistry, microbial genetics and artificial intelligence. Of course, I might have got the help anyway in a university organised along departmental lines, but it makes it easier if you meet people at coffee every morning. However, some more permanent research collaborations have developed, for example between psychologists and biologists studying hearing, and between biologists and biochemists studying development.

As I have hinted already, I have doubts about how far university science can or should be planned, and how far it should be directed towards practical ends. On the planning side, we have tried to identify important research topics, and we have appointed people whose research interests are likely to overlap. Nowadays, one needs groups of people working together: it is hard to make progress alone. We have also tried to get the maximum benefit, in teaching and research, from the presence on the campus of the AFRC Unit of Nitrogen Fixation and the AFRC Insect Chemistry and Physiology

Group, and the MRC Units of Cell Mutation and of Perceptual and Cognitive Performance. However, despite my reluctance to allow practical utility to dominate research, I am amused to discover how many applications have emerged from research done in the School. These include, for example, the treatment of diabetes, the synthesis of artificial speech for communication with computers, the control of blood flukes, the preservation of the countryside, the treatment of dyslexia, the effects of badgers on agriculture, and the development of salt-tolerant rice. If one encourages fundamental research, practical applications will emerge, and most scientists are keen to see their work put to use.

As I complete this essay, I am conscious that tomorrow the School is having a party to celebrate its first 20 years, and at the same time, to mark my own retirement – not that I have any intention of retiring. Despite the frustrations, during the past five years, of the financial cuts, and the inevitable disappointments when colleagues leave to take posts elsewhere, I am not sorry I left London to come to Sussex, nor too disappointed about the way it has worked out.

10
Design for the Twenty-first Century: The Evolution of Engineering

Fred Bayley

INTRODUCTION

To many, academic engineering is the ultimate contradiction. Even in its less pejorative uses 'academic' implies distance from reality or practice, and certainly from the marketplace. But engineering by definition must be practical, and, as engineers are constantly reminded in the present economic climate, it must be commercial; its products instantly saleable.

This contradication determines the philosophy of the dialectical debate among engineering educators operating at all levels, from the elementary to the most advanced. The debate in the end reduces to a question of time, both in the more obvious sense of how long should an engineering education require, and in the second and more difficult question, over what period should it, or can it, remain relevant. Thus a seven years' practical apprenticeship was once considered a *sine qua non* for engineering acceptability, with or without theoretical support, and pockets of this opinion can still be found in parts of the profession. Yet many engineers now at the peaks of successful careers were educated in the two-year college courses that had to suffice in the special circumstances of the Second World War, and which have recently again been mooted as suitable for the great majority of engineers (and even again, in a different form, for the most able students of all disciplines in the Green Paper (Cmnd. 9524) on higher education). Probably this form of the debate about engineering education is reconcilable, with a large majority accepting that a period between the extremes hypothecated above, of three or four years with an appropriate mix of the theoretical and practical, is somewhere near the ideal.

Less tractable is the second form of the chronological debate, for which the word much used by those charged with judging the value of postgraduate programmes is more apt – 'timeliness'. In essence, this is about what is the best form of education for engineers whose careers will on average last more than 40 years, a period in which technological changes of unpredictable magnitude and consequence will occur. It is usual to quote the computer to emphasise this point, but no less graphic examples are available in more traditional forms of engineering. Compare, for example, the two bridges which stand side by side over the Firth of Forth. These were built roughly an engineer's lifespan apart in time – some 70 years – a very small period in the long history of structural engineering which makes all the more dramatic the contrast between the massive railway bridge and the slender road bridge. Consider, too, since the two Forth bridges are concerned with different modes of transport, how technology has changed the distance attainable in a day's journey in the time between their building.

The dichotomy that has to be faced in planning the education of an engineer is between meeting the needs of the current market for the product and providing the knowledge and understanding that will remain relevant through a lifetime. The first view is exemplified by the remark of a member of the accreditation panel of one of the engineering institutions visiting us at Sussex, that he judged the value of a university engineering course by how quickly one of its graduates could make a profitable contribution to the company of which he was the senior engineer. This represents an extreme view, although one which is widely held in industry, members of which frequently criticise universities for not tailoring their courses to produce graduates with close knowledge of the current technology in a specialist branch of industry – an 'instantly saleable product' in the phrase of the opening paragraph.

The second view, no less widely held and perhaps beginning to prevail in the perceived climate of rapid technological change, is that an engineering education should be sufficiently broad at all levels to allow the recipients to adapt to changes in their careers, by giving them a thorough understanding of the fundamental principles that will remain relevant, as far as can currently be judged. Illustrations of these principles can, and must in an engineering course which is to be professionally acceptable, be applied to current examples of the technology; but it is the permanent role of the principles which must predominate rather than the transient role of the examples. Detailed knowledge of current technology, according to this view, must be obtained in practice after graduation.

This opinion is hedged, inevitably, with qualification, as proponents of the alternative will make clear. Which principles will remain relevant? The qualifying phrase of the previous paragraph, 'as far as can currently be judged', is not an answer which satisfies many. How broad is 'sufficiently broad'? Critics will quickly equate breadth with lack of depth, and depth will be seen by all as a crucial component of at least higher education.

These arguments will require a degree of compromise, no less at the postgraduate level of engineering education than the undergraduate and even earlier levels. At the 'taught' postgraduate level the argument can be less fierce, for here, where postgraduate can be equated almost with post-experience, the *raison d'être* must be to apply principles to current technology. At the research level, however, the engineering dichotomy is clear and concerns the closeness to or remoteness from current practice of the investigations. It can be forcefully argued on the one hand that it is the special role of the universities to conduct research far removed from immediate application. On the other hand, academic engineering must surely be concerned with application, and commercial application at that, for otherwise it is no different from the pure sciences – the pursuit of knowledge for its own sake. Again a compromise must be sought and it will involve the 'timespan of application' – the time to eventual commercial adoption of the knowledge the research programme produces. There is much room for different views on what is the appropriate period.

In the University of Sussex, we have had the great, and probably increasingly rare, privilege of creating a totally new academic engineering activity. In this essay, our attempts to reach the inevitable compromises between the extremes of view represented above are described, for both our teaching and research activities. The experience we have gained may be of interest to others, as we all try to forecast what the future might hold for engineering; remembering, too, that many of our present students will still be professionally active in the second quarter of the twenty-first century.

DEVELOPMENT OF UNDERGRADUATE COURSES

The decision by the founders of the University to organise the academic structure into Schools of Studies rather than separate departments had a profound effect upon the nature of the education offered, and not least in engineering. As the physicists have demonstrated for the natural sciences, and the sociologists would confirm, fission is a natural process more easily achieved than fusion. In higher education this is demonstrated by the plethora of autonomous specialist departments which have advantages for academic staff, as former colleagues who have gone to Chairs elsewhere have reported back, often with apparent relief. This is because courses can be planned with only the needs of the individual department in mind. Complete autonomy is, of course, impractical, for there is much common ground between even specialist subjects in the pure and applied sciences and interdepartmental teaching is essential. Organisation into coherent Schools of Studies enables full advantage to be taken of this common ground by arranging that such teaching is divided across the School in the early terms.

The Foundation Course
This arrangement of the early basic material into a common foundation course has special advantages for engineering education. As the boundaries between the traditional specialities become ever less clearly defined, successful graduate engineers must increasingly be prepared to understand the principles of specialisms beyond their own. There are also two more immediate advantages to such an arrangement. First and less tangible, the problems of minor (a euphemism for second-

138

class in the mind of the specialist) subjects is avoided. 'Thermodynamics for Electrical Engineers' connotes a less than crucial subject taught (often by new and inexperienced teachers, as we can all testify) to largely uninterested specialists; whereas, as part of a common engineering foundation course, the relevance and importance to teacher and student is clear. The second advantage of School-wide planning of a foundation course is doubly important to engineering, students of which have had to make their deliberate choice of this as a subject to study usually without much idea of what is entailed, since there is little engineering in secondary schools. A common foundation course allows a decision regarding specialisation to be deferred until students have experienced the contributions of the different specialists to their basic engineering education.

Acceptance of these advantages of a common engineering foundation course does not aid the resolution of the crucial questions which the practice raises: What should be the topics covered in the common course, and how far can complete commonality last into a full and professionally acceptable undergraduate education?

When the School of Engineering and Applied Scicenes was founded in 1965 at Sussex the intention was that it should comprise four activities equating approximately with separate departments in other universities. These were Electrical Engineering (to include Electronic and Computer Engineering), Materials Science, Mechanical Engineering (later to include Structural and then Civil Engineering) and Operational Research. The common foundation course that was agreed between these subjects, and which spanned the first six terms of the three-year honours degree course is shown as Table 1. The relatively small amount of the applied sciences in this course, especially in the first year, still reflected the hopes of the founders of the University in the earliest days for a two-term Preliminary course common to the whole of the sciences, which offered the assumed attraction of allowing students to defer decisions even between Schools of Studies until well into their undergraduate careers. This hope foundered with the creation of the School of Biological Sciences with its differing student mathematical background and

Table 1

First year:		
Term 1	Term 2	Term 3
Physics	Physics	Engineering analysis
Mathematics	Mathematics	Electrical engineering
Engineering science	Engineering science	Materials
Second year:		
Term 4	Term 5	Term 6
Mathematics	Materials	Numerical analysis
Electrical engineering	Electrical engineering	Social studies and
Mechanical engineering	Mechanical engineering	management (double)

requirements, compounded later after the introduction of engineering by the further differences between the pure and applied scientists.

The course shown in Table 1 was designed to give both the breadth of knowledge considered essential to the modern engineer, irrespective of final specialisation, and to lay a foundation for the in-depth studies appropriate for the final year of an honours degree. Fundamental changes to this initial structure were implemented, however, following two major reviews of its operation, the first in 1975 and the second in 1981. These changes were engendered by two quite separate factors. First, and largely the cause of the changes in 1975, was an almost abstract consideration, but one which appeared to be pose real problems to even the best students. This was the very sharp discontinuity in depth and breadth of course between the first two years and the final year, in which only topics associated with a student's intending special-isation – Electronic Engineering, Mechanical Engineering and so on – were studied. Thus the principal change introduced in 1975 was a 'tapering' of the courses, from the broad and entirely common foundation work to the totally specialist final year. This was achieved by reducing the span of the completely common course from six terms to four, by increas-ing the engineering content of the first two terms (at the expense of physics), while continuing a reduced core curricu-lum of common subjects to the end of the second year. In the fifth and sixth terms, however, students were permitted to select optional courses to reflect their likely choice of final-year specialisation and to supplement the core subjects. By this means some, but not all, final-year options were closed, and a deeper preparation for the final-year specialist topics was obtained through the 'selection' courses.

The second factor which led to a major review of courses, and especially the 1981 changes, is the continuous pressure in any subject, arts as well as science, to enlarge syllabuses to include new developments. The well-known explosion of computing power has had its effect on syllabuses, and will continue to do so, as will be seen in the final section of this essay. This effect arises both directly through the now essential requirement for all scientists and technologists to have an awareness of hardware potentialities and a familiarity with relevant software, and also indirectly through the changes produced in analytical and predictive capabilities in many other subjects. In more traditional and perhaps less well-known areas continuing changes also occur. Heat transfer as a subject, for example, dramatically affected by the computer in its predictive potential, in its own right has changed in status in most branches of engineering. Fifteen years ago it was barely visible in any undergraduate engineering syllabus, but even for electronic engineers heat transfer is now accepted as a core subject and a specialist final-year option for mechanical engineers. Thus although some material becomes obsolescent and can be dropped, it is the continuing experience of all educationalists that syllabuses grow, and the resulting pressures on the Sussex engineering foundation course proved irresistible. This was despite the closure of the Materials Science Subject Group following the 1981 retrenchment in the university sector, and the continuing of Operational Research as essentially a postgraduate subject. Table 2 shows the foundation course agreed between the two remaining principal groups, Electrical, Electronic and Computer Engineering, and Mechanical and Civil Engineering, for the academic year 1984/85. The contrast with the original form is striking, but there remain nevertheless continuing pressures for change. At the time of writing these are such as to require urgent consideration of a reduction of the common foundation course to three terms.

Table 2

First year		
Term 1	Term 2	Term 3
Fluid mechanics & heat transfer	Dynamics	Engineering thermodynamics
Statics	Electromagnetics	Linear engineering systems
Electric circuits	Instrumentation & circuits	Electrical machines
Software engineering	Digital electronics	Microprocessors
Engineering mathematics	Applied programming	Materials in engineering
	Engineering mathematics	Engineering mathematics

Second year	
Term 4	Terms 5 & 6
Structural mechanics	Management
Feedback control	Mathematics
Electronic signal systems	+ 4 specialist
Management	selection courses
Technical communication	
Engineering mathematics	

The Final Year

For all the engineering disciplines at Sussex, the final year is devoted solely to the specialist choice of Major subject. Even so, the breadth of modern engineering requires that there must still be some selectivity between topics if these are to be studied in depth. Preferably, this selection should be made by the students to reflect their own interests and preferences, but the pressures of expanding syllabuses referred to in the previous section (to say nothing of the not always understanding and far-sighted accreditation requirements of the professional engineering institutions) have tended to reduce the range of choice available to a student. Further, in the intensive three-year British engineering course, which despite all the pressures to have lengthened is likely to remain the norm, it is difficult to give students in their first two years adequate experience of the open-ended type of problem which typifies engineering in the real world. Thus a substantial part of the final year timetable must be given to design and research projects.

Assessment of student performance in the final year, and indeed throughout the earlier years, is still mainly by unseen papers. Although no convincingly fairer means of academic assessment has been devised, such papers have been the butt of constant criticism, probably since education began. Practising engineers, especially, make caustic comments about the contrast between the typical examination question, with its single perfect answer warranting full marks, and the problems of practical engineering to which there is an infinity of answers, none of them justifying full marks. However, continuous assessment, through reports from laboratories and tutorial classes, is used in the first two years to supplement examination information. In the final year, in particular, dissertations reporting the design and research projects, based upon and as far as possible representing real engineering problems, weigh heavily in the determination of degree class.

RESEARCH

An MSc course in Energy Studies is currently run by the physicists, chemists and engineers at Sussex. An MSc in Control Engineering was operated as an interesting experiment jointly with University College, Bangor and the University of Warwick for the first ten years after the opening of the Engineering School at Sussex, but this lapsed, as with so many such courses, when the demand from students of quality did not warrant the commitment of resources involved. Shorter post-experience courses, especially in computing, and electronics, have continued to be better supported. Longer diploma courses, and possibly Master's courses, based on these subjects are currently under examination. These will be related to integrated manufacturing systems, discussed more fully in the final section of this essay. But to date the postgraduate programme in engineering at Sussex has been predominantly concerned with research.

The judgements that must be made in defining engineering research programmes within a university were remarked upon in the opening section and in particular the perceived 'time-span of application'. Of course, worthwhile university research can be conducted at both ends of the spectrum of possibilities. After a serious accident, for example, academic expertise can be put to urgent use to try to explain the cause.

Equally, some research programmes in the applied sciences offer little hope of application, certainly commercial application, within the foreseeable future, and some of the more esoteric energy-saving projects come to mind in this connection. Generally, however, there are gaps in engineering knowledge and understanding, often indicated by current practice, which if filled within 5–10 years – the so-called strategic timescale – offer the prospect of commercial application; that is, adoption into the design of engineering products intended for sale into the market. With few notable exceptions, this view can be used to judge the suitability of an engineering research programme, and has determined the nature of nearly all research in the School of Engineering and Applied Sciences at Sussex.

Having accepted this guideline for acceptability of a proposed engineering research programme – it is hoped with some flexibility of attitude at the upper end of the timescale – the question, from which we can never be far removed in the current economic climate, arises of how the programme is to be funded. The days of the well-found laboratory may not quite have gone, but providing such a facility in present-day institutions of higher education does not leave much financial margin, so additional funding must be sought for even those projects satisfying most obviously our criterion of acceptability. And here the academic engineers meet their Scylla and Charybdis (or Catch-22, depending upon their literary tastes).

If the proposal is so certain of being commercially exploitable in the suggested timescale, surely an appropriate industrial organisation will fund the programme? If the uncertainties deter industry, should not the peer-groups who make the funding judgements on academic bids for research support – and in the case of engineering, with extensive advice from industrial members and assessors – be equally deterred?

It is not a solution to this paradox to hope that the Research Councils will be prepared to take greater risks than industry, for many of the most supportive companies have more resources for speculative ventures than the Councils. Equally, past success of a supplicant research group in attracting funds, especially from industry, apparently cannot be used to guide the judges of an application for it has recently been influen-

144

tially suggested that such funds are more likely to have been made available for 'hack' work – an aphorism for research of less than adequate scientific content. And here the academic engineers become more acutely aware of their contradictory existence. So many engineering problems, and often the most critical to industry, are not easily solved by innovative scientific methods. Often they simply require extensive routine testing – the 'stamp-collecting', so properly eschewed by academics. On the other side, a solution to another type of problem may not be adaptable to the design procedures feasible in an industrial situation – every design-draughtsman, despite his modern computer support, may not have access to a powerful machine like a Cray for routine calculations. With these additional constraints academic engineers may feel that the mythological monsters of Scylla and Charybdis or the aviators' dilemma in *Catch 22* offer degrees of freedom which they can only envy.

Despite all this, it is our experience at Sussex that the present system of support for engineering research works well, from sources both within and external to the University. We have received extensive support from many industrial companies, some not noted for their philanthropy (by which remark is intended a compliment rather than the reverse). This work it is believed has enhanced engineering and scientific knowledge and understanding (measured by published work) and to the advantage of the companies; and although the latter is for them to judge rather than we academics, continued support over long periods encourages us in that belief. (This statement, incidentally, does not in any way contradict the timespan criterion discussed at length above, for successful research can continue to make discernible future related problems.)

A matter not so far considered may be raised by the brief reference above to published work, and this concerns confidentiality. This should rarely pose a problem in academic–industry relations as discussed here, for the need for commercial confidentiality lies more often in the final application of the research than in the medium-term principles which properly should be the subject of academic engineering research. At Sussex there have been examples of companies in severe competition in the commercial world outside cooperating in common research programmes, taking results from the same test rigs. In this respect, the Cooperative Grant Scheme of the Science and Engineering Research Council has, in our experience, played a key part in encouraging such cooperation between industrial companies, the Council itself and the University, and, indeed, in circumventing the potential difficulties discussed at length here which could constrain the research work of the academic engineer. And here now perhaps the apparent contradiction of the term itself can be finally repudiated.

THE FUTURE

One of the more pointless of perpetual arguments has been about what is meant by the term 'engineer', and the only justification for adding to the debate here is to make quite clear what should be the role of the engineering graduate. He or she should 'be a person who by education and experience is able to design for sale a device to fulfil a specified function'. The commercial aspect of engineering has been highlighted in this text and certainly exclusion of the two words 'for sale' or their equivalent in such a definition changes its nature totally. One of the many criticisms that have been made of British engineers, particularly compared with their international competitors, has been neglect of the crucial need to sell their products. Whether this neglect springs from the British traditional desire to separate education from commerce, evidence of which can still be found in educational institutions from primary school to university, or whether the neglect springs from a century and a half of sellers' markets, provide an excellent basis for another pointless argument. It only matters that in the future the need to sell engineering products is clear to all, practising engineers and those concerned with education.

If the verb 'to sell' could once have been overlooked in defining the role of an engineer, the other key-word could never have been: engineering must be concerned with design. Yet this word, chosen deliberately because of its importance

146

for the title of this essay, occurs nowhere in describing the first two years of the undergraduate courses, and only rarely elsewhere in this text. This can only be justified by observing that good design is not possible until principles are understood and, less acceptably, because design (good or otherwise) is difficult to teach and research; indeed, an arguable point of view is that 'difficult' should be replaced by 'impossible'.

Whatever the title of this section – The Future – contains, it must include the emergence by whatever means of continuing generations of designers, for however firm the intent to sell into commercial markets, this objective can only follow good design. But it is the continuing experience of British engineering companies, at least in the older manufacturing industries, that the average age of their designers increases steadily; few young people, even if they enter it, stay in this quintessential engineering activity. Academic institutions must take their share of the blame for this situation, for they can justly be criticised for emphasising analysis rather than synthesis, or design, in their syllabuses. It is a partial defence only that principles can best be taught by analysis, but more persuasive to believe that the final word of the preceding paragraph is not totally flippant. Certainly, it is impossible to teach design without extensive practice, and in the past, in a three-year course, there has been insufficient time for this practice to be made available. However, just as it has changed many other judgements of what is possible, the computer offers the prospect of allowing adequate design practice in a much shorter time than did the traditional designer's tools of drawing board, T-square and a chisel-edged pencil. In the future, the very near future, academic institutions must seize the opportunities offered by computer-aided design (CAD) to direct some of their brightest students to becoming first-class designers.

With CAD increasingly is associated CAM (computer-aided manufacture) the last word of which phrase appears, shamefully and significantly, only once before in this text, and then in anticipation of this section. Manufacture, or production engineering, has always been the poor relation to other technologies, in Britain at least. This is another example of the traditional separation in our society between education and commerce, between the intellectual and the artisan; for after all, even the designer, no less than the analyst, can have intellectual pretensions but, we are inclined to believe, surely not the manufacturer of an artefact.

If Britain is to continue as a major manufacturing nation this attitude must change. Some would argue that it is already too late. Such pessimism can be countered, however, by the observation that young people are to be found in the design offices of our newer industries, and hence the qualification about design offices in the older manufacturing industries two paragraphs above. If Britain's industrial base cannot survive on computers alone, computers can allow that in our colleges and universities good design and its concomitant, efficient manufacture, can now, and must be, effectively taught to engineers for all industries. It is recognition of such changing needs in technology that will require educational institutions continuously to adapt and adjust their strategies, as we have sought to do in the School of Engineering and Applied Sciences at the University of Sussex.

11

The Queen of the Sciences: Mathematics at Sussex

Bernard Scott

Of all the Major subjects being taught in the University of Sussex when we started on our own site in 1962, Mathematics is the only one which would have been available in a new university had one been founded in 1762. Of the much wider range of Major subjects being taught in 1986 doubtless many of the trendier ones will have disappeared by 2186. The one certainty is that Mathematics will continue to be a Major subject if the University is still in business in 2186, and that some of the present Major subjects will continue, if at all, merely as special mathematical topics.

The position of mathematics on the Science side of a university is a somewhat equivocal one. This was beautifully illustrated at one of our early gatherings of schoolteachers where we were, to put it crudely, trying to sell the Science side of our new University. After an impassioned speech from Roger Blin-Stoyle on science and the devotion to it of himself and his colleagues, combined with some very stirring stuff on the physics which was lying in wait for them to discover, I followed in a somewhat different vein. My line was that, contrary to general belief, mathematics was *not* a highly impersonal subject, but was actually the most personal of all the sciences. We mathematicians were not concerned with mathematics waiting to be discovered: our problem was that we were confronted with mathematicians whose personal potential had to be realised as fully as possible, and that only in this way could research (or any other activity) in mathematics be advanced.

Worthwhile research in mathematics is not (as in other sciences) to be achieved by industry, patience, talented leadership, teamwork and a reasonable level of technical skill in the team: it involves a real creative process which, as a recent SERC report makes clear, is a matter for individual activity or collaboration between very small numbers (usually two) of people. Since Newton's time England has usually been one of the world's outstanding countries for mathematical achievement. At present, with Russia and France, we are second only to the United States and, within this country, Sussex has in its short life made a significant contribution, as is clear from a ranking table based on the same SERC report. The camaraderie of the international mathematical community has meant a great deal to us, especially in our earliest days. Many of the world's most distinguished mathematicians have assisted us with their interest and goodwill, and above all by their presence on the campus. The University has shown its appreciation of the assistance of three of our most persistently helpful Visiting Professors (Segre, Serrin and Bondi) by conferring honorary degrees on them.

Now while much of this volume deals with research developments at Sussex, few of its readers will wish to learn about (or even be able to understand) the details of what has been, and is being, achieved in mathematical research at Sussex. Most readers are more likely to be concerned with our treatment of our undergraduates and what is done in Sussex to develop their potential. This is something which, as will appear later, is not distinct from the promotion of research but even so it has its own importance, especially for intending students. One of the problems here is that the range of mathematical talent is enormously wider than in other subjects, and even among professional mathematicians the gap between competent skilled practitioners of international standing and the towering geniuses of mathematics is greater than in other disciplines. Which helps to explain why the appointment in 1966 of a 26-year-old (now Sir John Kingman) to a Sussex Chair of Mathematics was accepted as reasonable and welcome by his immediate colleagues, even though the great majority of them were older than him, but regarded with considerable suspicion at the time outside the Mathematics Subject Group.

The needs of undergraduate training complement rather than conflict with the development of research. In considering in 1961–62 the establishment of a Research School in Mathematics there were two outstanding points to bear in mind. The first one was that, despite the existence of brilliant Schools in other places at other times, no university in Britain had ever for long challenged the mathematical dominance of Cambridge. And the reason for this was a very simple one. Cambridge has far and away the best mathematical undergraduates, and this has always kept them ahead even at times when other universities might have had the more creative younger staff. (It remains to be seen whether this dominance will long survive the abolition of the scholarship system.) The second point was that the eminence, vitality and, above all, the outstanding leadership of the Manchester School in the late 1940s and the 1950s never made the impact on the country that it ought to have done. The prestige of this department abroad, and indeed in the mathematical trade at home, was never matched by a corresponding improvement in its student intake: they never seriously convinced the outstanding potential undergraduates or research students that this was the place to go to. Indeed, the potential customers may have been right to suspect that the department was more concerned with the research output of its staff than with the welfare of its undergraduates.

From an early stage the priorities of our Mathematics Subject Group were to get the best available staff and to build up the quality of the undergraduate intake, the first essential for which is to do a good job for the students who are actually there *and* to make sure that the schools know about it. We began with the assumption that any solidly-based creative mathematical institution must depend for its long-term stability on a balance between its research and its teaching functions. If the research (i.e. the overall quality of the faculty) is below the standards of the students there must be a decline in the quality of the intake. A research school which appears to be interested only in those undergraduates who are potential researchers necessarily alienates the bulk of its students, which again induces a decline in quality. And in the long run if the quality of the faculty is not approached by that of the undergraduates the staff will inevitably be drained away to places with better students. So a concern for the well-being of the students is not only important in itself but is an essential element in a long-term strategy for mathematical research.

In the cause of undergraduate recruitment we took much trouble in the early days to make contact with the schools. First of all, the public relations efforts of our first Vice-Chancellor and the various meetings of headmasters he organised to publicise the University's initial activities did a great deal to assist recruitment. We took a great deal of trouble to write personal (not stereotyped) letters to headmasters after interviewing candidates for admission. (The great spin-off from John Fulton's gatherings of headmasters was that the informal contacts made outside the formal sessions made it much easier to visualise the recipients of our letters as persons.) And much effort was put into making contact with teachers, especially through the Mathematical Association. Much of all this was done through social contacts at the Annual General Meetings which are held at different places in England and Wales, and where very good and helpful relations were also established with Her Majesty's Inspectors of Schools. We have also made strenuous local efforts. The creation of the Sussex Branch of the Mathematical Association was a consequence of the foundation of the University and the Mathematics Subject Group has continued to play a large part in its activities. The benefits of this to the Group were somewhat indirect since, although we did obtain some excellent students from local schools, we had no wish to rely on them as a source of recruitment. But the establishment in Brighton of a particularly successful junior branch of the Association (to be followed more recently by another one in Hastings) led to the formation of such branches in other parts of the country. As a result of this Walter Ledermann and I were invited to address meetings of sixth-formers (including several inaugural Branch meetings) in, *inter alia*, Birmingham, Bristol, Ipswich, Leeds, Reading and Sheffield. More recently, in collaboration with the Royal Institution, the local Mathematical Association has been running at the University, with considerable faculty assistance and the use of our mathematical laboratories, Saturday morning courses of so-called Master Classes for 14-year-olds at Sussex schools. The success of this can be gauged by the fact that in the last academic year, despite the dreadful winter, all 41 pupils who started on the course stayed till the end.

The main question being asked in the early days, by both the schools and the mathematical profession, was what kind of staff were we getting here? We were the first of the new universities to recruit and mathematicians at that time were in very short supply so there was a feeling in the trade that we might get no respectable staff at all. We were aiming from the beginning for a wide coverage of the mathematical field for a number of reasons. In the first place we wanted to provide the widest possible opportunities for our students. Next we wanted, in the interests of the University, to be in a position to collaborate with disciplines outside mathematics and physics. This meant that we needed, for instance, applied mathematicians with engineering interests and statisticians with biological interests as well as people expert in computing of all kinds. So our aim was first of all to acquire the services of outstanding mathematicians, in almost any field, when the opportunity arose (or could be made to arise), which naturally produced a wide spread of interests, and to make special efforts to recruit in statistics and numerical mathematics, these being the most useful subjects for both students and academic colleagues. This specialised recruitment was, in the circumstances of the time, almost a full-time job in itself: we were eventually very successful in statistics and managed adequately in numerical mathematics, but to have attempted such efforts in more than two fields would have been impractical. And, in any case, the personal nature of mathematical research does not call for large specialist groups as in some other sciences. Isolated individuals or small groups of people, unless overwhelmed by a large number of students, can gain far more from colleagues of similar talent in neighbouring fields than from less gifted people in their own. Indeed that kind of contact can cause research groups to crystallise out in ways which may well result in their doing better than if they had been recruited on a more specialised basis. Certainly in Sussex our very strong groups in algebra and differential equations have developed in this way, even though some specialised recruitment did later take place, with SERC support, in differential equations.

After more than 20 years we can take stock of what has been achieved in recruiting students and staff. Of course we have not, nor did we expect it, overtaken Cambridge in either respect but our achievement is none the less substantial. Measured by the usual A-level criteria we seem to have the best undergraduate intake on the Science side of the University, and better than all but the Computer Studies students on the Arts side. We have had some outstanding research students, some of whom have already acquired Chairs elsewhere and others whose theses were international sensations in their fields. And the quality of the faculty we recruited is illustrated by the following selection from their achievements. We have had two Fellows of the Royal Society (a much rarer achievement for mathematicians than for experimental scientists) and four Berwick Prizes (three Junior and one Senior) of the London Mathematical Society. One of the FRSs, also a Royal Medallist, has become successively Chairman of the Science and Engineering Research Council and Vice-Chancellor at Bristol, and another has become a Vice-Chancellor in Australia. Five of our number received internal promotion to Chairs and former members of faculty have moved on to Chairs at Oxford, London, Leiden, Warwick (2), Geneva, Bradford and Lecce. The pity of this is that we have not received the usual (and natural) reward for an outstanding nursery of talent, which is a continuous infusion of bright young colleagues, since we have been prevented (by financial stringencies) from replacing many of these brilliant young men whose careers have been so successfully forwarded at Sussex.

The tutorial philosophy of the University has been a help in dealing with the inevitable spread of talent among our undergraduates. Certainly our students in the lower third of the ability range (and every department necessarily has a lower third) do seem to get more out of their course (judged by the kind of activity they take up after leaving us) than those in the distinguished conventional department in which I served previously. (And a special tribute should be paid here to Tony Caston, the University's first Appointments Officer, who got the placing of our former students off to a splendid and imaginative start.) A mathematical degree is a very saleable qualification and our graduates have done very well. And the Major/Minor approach of Sussex courses (though we have now breached it for abler students who wish to confine themselves to mathematics) has great advantages for individual students and also for the community at large. Mathematical ability is needed in many activities and not only is it desirable that many talented mathematicians should be employed outside the mathematical trade, but many students on mathematics courses acquire valuable skills which, while not necessarily remarkable in a purely mathematical context, would appear outstanding to practitioners of other disciplines. Our ME (Mathematics Major/Economics Minor) course has turned some excellent mathematicians into first-rate academic economists who could not have been trained in a conventional economics (or mathematics) department. And the MCS (Mathematics with Computer Science) course provides a far more sophisticated mathematics training than conventional degree courses in Computer Science. The recent appointment to the University's new Chair of Computing Science gives prospects of very interesting developments here.

The essential approach to Mathematics courses in Sussex is that we do not try to teach our students all the mathematics they may later need. Quite apart from the limitations on the amount of information which can be imparted in three years, the inevitable changes in technology make it impossible to forecast what mathematics our students may require 15 or 20 years after graduation. So we concentrate, in the first two years of the course, on providing the basic mathematical training which will enable them to learn further skills they may later require and on giving them an introduction to useful mathematics. We build on this foundation in the third year by providing a wide range of options to suit the tastes and the abilities of individual students. The useful material of the first two years involves not merely essential algebra, analysis and classical applied mathematics, but also statistics, numerical mathematics and computing, and those who are especially interested in these topics can carry them further in the third year. In particular the MS (Mathematics with Statistics) course provides the essentials of a statistical training. Of course, all this requires a wide spread of interests among the faculty and, with the large faculty numbers initially allocated to us, we were well equipped. In the first year or two, while faculty numbers were small, we had problems here which were mitigated by the didactic virtuosity and wide interests of many members of faculty. Now that several key persons have departed without, for the most part, being replaced the Subject Group is dependent on the versatility of those who are left and the part-time teaching contribution of retired colleagues. In this way no subject that we wish to teach has to be left out, but the statistical teaching is perhaps rather hard pressed.

A recent development which has proved exciting for both students and staff is our extensive provision of microcomputing facilities in mathematics teaching laboratories, which provide excellent facilities. We have a large number of BBC machines with adequate peripherals (disc-drives and printers) and a newly installed networking system offers facilities for teaching and learning which are already notable and will be great fun to exploit further. The laboratories are proving very popular with students who enjoy free access to the equipment when it is not required for formal teaching and who show no hurry to leave, nor are they pressed to do so, at the conclusion of their laboratory sessions. The laboratory has produced a ferment of ideas about teaching in which there has been eager cooperation among many members of faculty with widely separated professional interests, and the interaction here between the applied mathematicians and some of the very abstract pure mathematicians has been an eye-opener.

12

An Epitome of Education

Norman MacKenzie and Michael Eraut

Three men ensured that education would figure significantly in the plans for Sussex. William Stone, Director of Education in Brighton, had done more than anyone to bring the first of the new universities to the town, and he was a member of the Academic Advisory Committee which oversaw its early years. John Fulton came from a Balliol noted for A. D. Lindsay's social concerns, and Lindsay's own transition from an Oxford college to Keele was both an example and a challenge to him when he reached the virgin pastures of Stanmer Park. And in Asa Briggs, whose academic radicalism ran all the way from the groves of academe to the schoolroom and the W.E.A. class, he found the ideal complement. The fundamental ideas came from this triumvirate. With the appointment of Boris Ford, who came to Sussex by a route that ran from the Army Bureau of Current Affairs through Rediffusion TV and the Chair of Education at Sheffield, they found their energetic and often controversial instrument.

As early as 1959 some of the founding fathers were asking what role education might play in the new University and also what role the University as a whole might play in the wider educational community. But there was much else to do, so it was not until 1963 that the University began to translate some general ideas about education into specific proposals.

Asa Briggs set out the details in a paper written in January 1963. It was, he claimed, 'at least as radical (and constructive) as the scheme of undergraduate education which we have evolved', and it would guarantee that education would be central rather than peripheral to the life of the University. There was, first, to be a distinct place for education in the undergraduate curriculum, but the courses were to define a field of study rather than provide, like the BEd later offered by the teacher training colleges, a combination of academic work with the required professional component. Secondly, Sussex would establish its own postgraduate courses in education and social work for graduates requiring specific qualifications. Thirdly, the proposed School of Education would be the focus for the colleges and schools throughout Sussex, validating the college courses for intending teachers and collaborating to provide in-service training for those already in the profession. Fourthly, taking over the region's extramural programme from Oxford, it would develop an extensive and diverse offering in the field of continuing education. Finally, it would infuse these varied activities with research interests which would initially concentrate upon the problems of adolescence, educational innovation and higher education itself.

Even at Sussex, so dedicated to novelty, this coherent vision was ahead of its time. Patrick Corbett, urging the still small Senate to contain its doubts about including education anywhere in the undergraduate curriculum, spoke in March 1963 of 'the atmosphere of enterprise and expectation' created by Briggs' paper, and criticised 'the old attitudes towards education which naturally still fill our colleagues' minds'. That scepticism was never crippling but it was never wholly eliminated. It was less evident in matters that fell within the accepted external boundaries of a Department of Education and most assertive whenever an innovation (such as new ideas about teaching) seemed to threaten academic conventions and prerogatives elsewhere in the University.

The first step, which was the creation of the School of Educational Studies,* raised predictable objections. Members of Senate asked whether education could properly be a degree subject, whether it should be married to a recognised discipline in a double Major, whether it would be offered only to intending teachers and social workers, and how it might relate to the pattern of undergraduate teaching already established for the humanities and social sciences. Yet it was precisely this pattern that made it relatively easy for Asa Briggs and Boris

---

* During its first year this was called the School of Education and Social Work.

Ford (whose appointment as Professor of Education was reported to Senate in March 1963) to place the new School alongside the four which had already been agreed. The School of Educational Studies only needed to provide its own group of Contextual courses as authenticated academic Majors were already developed for the four existing Schools of Studies. It thus came to life fully-fledged, instead of going through a slow process of developing a separate repertoire of Major courses. By 1965 it was offering six Contextuals: *Education and Society, Personality and Social Groups, Social Structure and Social Change, Developmental Psychology, Philosophy: Thought and Action,* and *Community Studies and Social Work.* The first entrants could take Majors in English, Geography, History, Philosophy, Psychology, Religious Studies and Sociology; and other subject specialisms soon followed. Only the Psychology Major was new.

THE NEW PGCE COURSE

Asa Briggs and Boris Ford had originally advocated an integrated four-year course for training teachers and social workers, and were particularly attracted by the proposal at York whereby professional practice began in the third year. But the Sussex curriculum precluded this in either science or modern languages; and the staffing to run two separate schemes was never forthcoming. So while it was possible for many Sussex undergraduates to take Education Contextual courses in the School of Educational Studies, professional training was confined to a separate Postgraduate Certificate in Education (PGCE).

At first, subject teaching specialists were brought in from Brighton College of Education to complement the general education and social science expertise of the University. Then, in accordance with Asa Briggs' original emphasis on the role of subject teaching in professional training, a series of 'E' appointments were made. This new kind of teacher educator was to combine the teaching of a subject on BA and BSc courses with preparing graduates to teach their subject in secondary schools. They had to have both sufficient academic expertise in their subject to be fully acceptable to their colleagues and sufficient school teaching experience to be credible as teacher trainers. Since two-thirds of their time was to be spent with their subjects, there was no question of their being regarded as 'second-class citizens' in the academic community. Remarkably, such people were found. Though their dual role has proved unusually stressful, their special contribution has continued to play an important part in Education at Sussex.

Meanwhile, a new school-based format for teacher training was tried in 1965–66 with the second cohort of PGCE students, using a pattern similar to the new Diploma in Social Work. Instead of the traditional block teaching practice in their second term, a small experimental group of students started in school three days a week from the beginning of the autumn term, then continued their teaching practice throughout the year. Greater responsibility was given to practice schools, some of whose teachers were paid to give additional tutorials on site. In March 1967 this newly christened 'tutorial school scheme' was adjudged to be giving the better results. Moreover, school-based students found the psychological and sociological aspects of the course more comprehensible and useful, since from the start they were able to see their practical implications; while college-based students still felt the theory part was somehow unreal. It was resolved to change the whole course to the new scheme from 1968/69 with the subject pedagogy role being taken by a unique combination of University E-tutors and school-based teacher tutors.*

THE SCHOOL OF EDUCATION

Regional consultations about a School of Education based on the Robbins recommendations began with Boris Ford's appointment. An early meeting with college Principals and

---

* A description and evaluation of this new scheme is provided by Lacey and Lamont, *Partnership with Schools: an experiment in teacher education*, University of Sussex Education Area Occasional Paper 5 (1976).

Chief Education Officers led to a Senate paper in February 1964, which described the intended School of Education as 'a federal body within the University composed of the University School of Education and Social Work and the Colleges of Education'. Further progress had to await the government's decisions on the Robbins proposals. Then in December 1964 the new Labour government, under strong pressure from the local education authorities, resolved not to assimilate the colleges into the autonomous university system. Thus began the binary policy which was to divide and confuse higher education for the following 20 years. While every college was linked to one or other of the universities which had an Institute of Education, making those universities responsible for the academic oversight of college syllabuses and examinations, administrative and financial control was left in the public or local authority sector. Such a policy produced endless conflicts of interest and policy, even where, as in Sussex, all concerned were genuinely committed to cooperation; but at least the academic relationships could become collegial and mutually beneficial.

Boris Ford's encouragement of self-expression and diversity was peculiarly relevant to the local situation – it would have been impossible to impose a standard academic pattern on three general colleges (Bishop Otter at Chichester, Brighton and Eastbourne), the Seaford College of Home Economics, Chelsea College of Physical Education and Brighton College of Art. His enthusiasm not only helped the colleges to move rapidly to the new four-year BEd, which was first awarded in 1968: it also laid the foundations for their later diversification into general degrees of higher education which the University was to assist with guidance and validation. The long and cordial partnership between the University and the colleges, broken eventually by a succession of mergers and closures, often gave glimpses of what might have been achieved if the Robbins proposals had been implemented.

The other major obligation of a School of Education was the provision of in-service courses and other support for serving teachers. While this was stressed in correspondence from DES, it was some time before the necessary resources were forthcoming. George Allen was appointed in 1965 as a second Professor of Education to assist with BEd responsibilities; but it was not until 1969 that David Burrell was appointed as Staff Tutor to organise a short-course programme. Attention then turned to the provision of library and laboratory facilities, and to planning a BEd degree for serving teachers. This degree was jointly designed, managed and taught by the University, the five colleges and the Art Education department of Brighton Polytechnic. It consisted of a part-time preparatory year followed by a full-time year, had a strong orientation towards practical curriculum development work in schools, and was designed to build on and use the accumulated professional knowledge of the experienced teachers who took it. All seven institutions contributed to the interdisciplinary education components; and special subjects were located in those colleges best able to support them.

THE CENTRE FOR CONTINUING EDUCATION

Asa Briggs produced a further position paper on continuing education in February 1966. This stressed the need for the whole University to be involved in continuing education and the danger of creating a separate 'extramural department' of a conventional kind before the University was ready to assume this responsibility. By 1968, however, he felt able to set up a Centre for Continuing Education to act as the focus of the University's involvement with Manny Eppel, a University colleague with long experience as an extramural tutor who shared his vision, as Director-Designate. Manny Eppel masterminded the establishment of the new Centre, which was granted Responsible Body status for East Sussex by the DES from 1969; and, then in the early 1970s for Crawley and Horsham in West Sussex. Again, something like the E-post system was adopted, with tutors being employed for two-thirds of their time on continuing education and for one-third on internal teaching in their parent subjects. Alongside this DES-funded liberal non-vocational, community-based programme, Manny Eppel developed a range of initiatives in post-experience, professional education, most notably for doctors, social workers, magistrates, police officers and trades union officers. University colleagues contributed to both programmes according to their expertise.

THE CENTRE FOR EDUCATIONAL TECHNOLOGY

The final part of Asa Briggs' programme for Education at Sussex was research. Characteristically, both he and Boris Ford had advocated that higher education itself should be the object of study; and self-evaluation and innovation in methods of teaching and learning were suggested as possible foci. This aspiration was to be realised in an unexpected manner. One of us (Norman MacKenzie), a Lecturer in Sociology with considerable experience of the mass media, chaired a Senate working party on the use of television in the University, then got external funding from the Rank Organisation to implement some of its recommendations, together with those of parallel working parties on language laboratories and programmed learning. A Centre for Educational Technology (CET)* was formed in February 1966 with MacKenzie as Director and Hywel Jones as his deputy, and UGC recognition as a high activity centre.† Audiovisual services were organised, television facilities developed and a language laboratory installed. Several research grants were obtained and, with LEA support, work was begun with local schools. This remarkably rapid growth began to be perceived as a threat by those in mainstream education and eventually the Media Service section was transferred to the library, while CET retained its academic role of research and development, teaching and consultancy for use in a wider, more cooperative context.

---

* For its first two years, this was called the Centre for Academic Services.
† Its ideas were given wide circulation in MacKenzie, Eraut and Jones, *Teaching and Learning: an introduction to new methods and resources in higher education* (UNESCO, 1970).

CREATION OF AN EDUCATION AREA

The formation of a new Education Area in 1971 would have seemed a most unlikely development when Boris Ford arrived in 1963. For then the focus was largely on the integration of professional training with normal undergraduate work, in marked contrast to the largely postgraduate emphasis of the Education Area. So what were the factors which caused this change? Ostensibly, it was a building. The technical facilities of the Centre for Educational Technology – television studio, film facilities, photographic unit, sound studio – needed a purpose-designed building; and this was recognised by Planning Committee in September 1967. It was also agreed that there was much to be gained by combining these with a home base for the School of Education, whose in-service facilities could be shared with PGCE students. These included science and mathematics laboratories, a creative area/experimental classroom for primary teachers, and a library. UGC finance was supplemented by grants from Esso for regional educational development facilities and from Reginald M. Phillips to house the research unit he endowed for the teaching of the deaf.

Another factor was the creation of an Arts Graduate School with education and social work divisions, thus formally separating professional training in Education, which was entirely postgraduate, from the undergraduate school that had now become the School of Cultural and Community Studies. The education graduate division was keen to expand its post-experience work at MA level, and for this it needed cooperation from CET.

All this happened at a time when the University was preparing its submission to the UGC for the next quinquennium; and during the course of these discussions the idea of a separate Education Area was born. Its components were to be the School of Education, the education graduate division and the Centre for Educational Technology. The newly formed Centre for Continuing Education was located in the same building but remained administratively independent. Continuity was guaranteed by Boris Ford becoming its first Chairman, and isolation was prevented by a considerable volume of cross-teaching with the other Areas. The input of E-appointments into Education was complemented by many members of the new Area continuing to teach in Arts, while Education teaching in Science began with the introduction of Education Minors. To chart the new Area's progress in detail would be a lengthy undertaking; but some of its problems and achievements over the ensuing 15 years are briefly discussed below.

CHANGING RELATIONSHIPS WITH THE COLLEGES

Only five months after the formation of the Education Area, the James Report was published, and ten months later, in December 1972, the government's inappropriately named White Paper, *Education: A Framework for Expansion*, in fact, heralded a period of major contraction in the teacher training system. The imperatives for the colleges of education were threefold: all but a few had to merge or close; they had to diversify by developing BAs to complement their BEds; and they eventually had to phase out their initial Certificate courses.

The University's response was rapid and sympathetic. It agreed to expand its validation role to include BAs by setting up a Colleges Advisory Board in December 1973. Under the successive chairmanship of Norman MacKenzie and Angus Ross it appointed an advisor for each college to organise the flow of proposals and the consultations with Subject Groups; developed policies for admissions, assessment, award of honours, etc.; and regularly reported to Senate. Meanwhile the School of Education developed a three-year BEd course without honours by enhancing the original Certificate courses. Though administrative support came from the Education Area, most of the academic burden fell on the college advisors and the members of Subject Groups in Arts and Science, who gave generous assistance in the development of new courses. Thus the colleges were able to accomplish this major academic transition 'among friends' and in time to admit students for the new BA and BEd awards in September 1975. The safety net provided by the University saved them from immediate closure, and offered some protection from institutional chaos.

The University saw this diversification as a means of improving higher education throughout Sussex and of replacing the old School of Education by a collegial partnership across the whole field. But a far more significant issue, which would have shifted the University's course towards the federated University of Sussex which Asa Briggs had envisaged ten years before, was the possible assimilation of Brighton College of Education, now on a splendid site opposite the University. The Senate, the College's Academic Board and the teachers' unions in Sussex all backed the idea. But, as at the time of Robbins, first Brighton then the new East Sussex Authority wished to maintain control. The College's merger with Brighton Polytechnic was agreed by the Secretary of State for Education and Science in March 1975, with the proposal that the University continue as the validating agency being given particular ministerial approval.

Those who devoted so much time to these discussions about new degree proposals and mergers during 1973 and 1974 can hardly have imagined that the process would continue for another five years. Internally, the Colleges Advisory Board was still seen as a stop-gap and an opportunity for the more conservative elements to keep sniping away in Senate. Reassurance on standards was difficult to provide for those who had not seen the quality of the best BEd work, until the first reports from external examiners arrived; and anxieties were voiced about the demands on the time of Subject Groups. The Registrar's paper on a 'final' structure for validation went through at least a dozen drafts between May 1974 and March 1977, when a Senate Validation Committee under the Pro-Vice-Chancellor was set up to replace the Colleges Advisory Board.

Externally, mergers and closures proceeded apace. In January 1977, Rendel Jones, Chief Education Officer for East Sussex, described in *Education* how the county was merging three colleges to form the East Sussex College of Higher Education at one end, while incorporating Brighton College of Education within the Polytechnic at the other. But the very same issue announced new DES proposals which put the whole scheme back in the melting-pot. Eventually, the Eastbourne complex was also merged with the Polytechnic and only the Chelsea School of Human Movement retained a separate identity. At the same time the West Sussex Institute of Higher Education was formed by merging Bishop Otter College, which was validated by the University of Sussex, with Bognor College, which was not. The Academic Board voted in June 1978 to transfer BEd validation to CNAA. Then Brighton Polytechnic followed in December 1978, against the wishes of the faculties concerned. Senate then agreed to cease validation; and the last students from affiliated institutions graduated in 1984.

What had been achieved by this 20-year relationship? The scale of the enterprise was rarely appreciated. Between 1966 and 1978 more than half of the University's awards were in Education, reaching a peak of just over 1600 in 1975; and in 1978 the 800 BEd degrees awarded exceeded the number of BAs. But, above all, it is the qualitative aspects which remain in the mind. Scholarship, diversity and professionalism were encouraged and supported throughout a period when college staff were first flooded by students then forced to fight for survival. There were no battles, only the shared aims of good courses, good teaching and a high quality of student work.

THE DEVELOPMENT OF MA COURSES

While the professional orientation of the Education Area was intended from the outset, the extent of its involvement with post-experience students was less predictable. Whereas in 1970, three-quarters of its postgraduate students were in initial training, this had fallen to a half by 1976, and in 1986 will be only 40 per cent (of whom about a third will be over 25). The main expansion has been in MA courses, particularly part-time, for which there is a considerable demand in Sussex and well beyond its borders. By 1981 there were over 100 part-time post-experience students taking MA and research degrees; and patterns of attendance have been worked out to suit them. Most courses combine one evening a week with summer schools or residential weekends, but some are able to use day-release.

The early development of a novel, school-based pattern for the PGCE was soon followed by a series of experiments with MA courses, which sought to find new ways of linking theory with practice by building on the accumulated professional know-how of post-experience students. They came expecting somehow to be able to apply 'our' theory to 'their' practice; and we had to avoid giving it to them in a way that made it 'ours' for ever. To acquire their own theory they had to learn to theorise about their own practice and hence to transform it: theory plucked 'off the shelf' would get put back up again once the course was over.

These experiments began with the Diploma in Educational Technology course, which combined seminars for discussing theoretical reading and personal experience with a series of school-based tasks. As the course developed, some tasks became more research-like and analytical while others were practical and developmental. Thus during the 1970s a group of MA courses evolved which focused on curriculum change: one in schools, one in higher and further education and one in Third World countries. Theory, methods workshops and fieldwork inquiry were used to develop students' capacities for analysing organisations and curricula in action. This was followed by seminars on the management of change, and on staff and curriculum development. Assessment was based on two minor projects and a final major project or dissertation. In many cases students' projects were carried out in their own institution or at the request of a client institution so their findings could be put to immediate use.

The first MA in Education course had been started by Mollie Adams in 1966 to prepare college of education lecturers for teaching education theory; but by the late 1970s when recruitment to colleges had virtually ceased, a radical rethink was needed. The courses which replaced it have proved increasingly relevant during the changes of the last five years. *Education and Society* examines education in its wider social context using a combination of social philosophy, sociology and anthropology. *Educational Policies and Decision-Making* studies the process of policy-making in LEAs and schools as well as at national level, the politics of the curriculum and ways in which policies are evaluated and implemented.

Yet another approach to the MA opportunity has been taken by *Language, the Arts and Education*. This invites creative work from the student and includes an autobiographical element, alongside more theoretical analyses of the nature of communication and the creative process. All three elements feed into an ongoing discussion about the nature and role of the arts in our society and how they should be supported in our educational system. *Women in Education* also includes an autobiographical element, together with social-scientific and historical analyses of gender as a dimension of teaching and learning, and of educational organisation and provision.

Then, finally, in recognition of the greater diversity and maturity of experienced professionals, an MA by *Independent Study* has been introduced. This comprises two minor projects and one major project, each separately tutored. It can be taken by almost any combination of full-time and part-time study. The flexibility offered to students is considerable but great care has to be taken over selection.

It is perhaps difficult for those who have not shared such an experience to realise how a mid-career course of this kind not only provides skills of immediate use but also enables professionals to learn more effectively in the future. They come to understand their past experience better, to bring it under critical control and put it to better use; and they learn to read their current experience more sensitively and at a deeper level. For members of faculty also, there is a similar gain. One of the privileges of teaching post-experience students is the amount one learns from them.

RESEARCH IN EDUCATION

Two styles of research were already in evidence when the Education Area was formed: a tradition of applied research and development in the curriculum was started by Michael Eraut and others within CET; and Colin Lacey, who came to direct an SSRC-funded evaluation of the PGCE course, was engaged in sociological research from a symbolic interactionist perspective. Soon Michael Eraut succeeded Norman Mac-Kenzie as Director of CET, while Colin Lacey on George Allen's retirement was appointed to a Chair incorporating a five-year, half-time appointment as Research Director at the Schools Council. When Boris Ford left for Bristol at Christmas 1973, his successor, Tony Becher, came from the Nuffield Foundation. This investment in research-oriented leadership met with considerable success and a substantial number of funded projects. For five successive years from 1972 to 1977 the University of Sussex topped the 'league table' for research in education, deriving about half of its income from external funds.

One early research emphasis was the design and evaluation of learning materials. The Continuing Mathematics Project published some 50 booklets for non-specialist mathematicians in the 16+ age group. The Sussex component of the Inter-University Biology Project published a substantial course of independent study for undergraduates comprising twelve books and audiovisual materials. Two curriculum projects for deaf children were based in the Phillips Unit; and a further project on the Structuring of Play in Infant Schools was funded by the Schools Council. More recently, primary science material and computer programs for teachers to design worksheets have continued this tradition.

A major research project on methods of evaluating curriculum materials, and involving collaboration with German and Swedish universities, received funding from the Volkswagen Foundation; and its results have been widely used abroad as well as in Britain. Indeed, evaluation has become something of a Sussex specialty. Grants for specific evaluations have been received throughout the last 15 years and several research projects have focused on new evaluation processes and techniques. Currently, four evaluation projects are in progress: pilot schools for the Certificate of Pre-Vocational Education; pilot test-bed schemes for the Youth Training Scheme; self-evaluation guidelines for youth leaders; and guidance on evaluating management courses.

When funding for curriculum development began to decline, much of the Area's project research took on a policy orientation. Three important projects in the late 1970s investigated *The Impact and Take-Up of Schools Council Projects* (Colin Lacey), *Accountability in Middle Years of Schooling* (Tony Becher and Michael Eraut) and *Falling Rolls in Secondary Schools*. This last project was directed by Eric Briault, who became a Visiting Professor at Sussex when he retired as Education Officer of ILEA. He is now assisting with Tony Bailey's project on management training; while Eric Hewton is co-directing the third successive joint research project with East Sussex Education Authority, on school-focused staff development. Two other areas where research is expanding are education in the Third World, where there have been close links with the Institute of Development Studies, and mid-career professional education.

Though funded research tends to capture the limelight, it forms only part of the picture. The Area reached its current number of just over 40 research students in 1978, and a steady flow of theses and student publications has been sustained. Members of faculty have frequently published findings from field research or library-based scholarship rather than funded projects, though the heavier loads following the cuts of 1981 make it increasingly difficult to find enough time. Four-fifths have published a book or directed a funded research project in the last five years; and few university departments can match that record.

NEW APPROACHES TO SHORT COURSE PROVISION

Throughout the period under review, many parts of the University organised courses and conferences for teachers of their subjects. The Education Group have sought to complement this by providing courses geared to the processes of change, evaluation and management. Its three fundamental principles evolved in the early days of CET, when two research projects conducted a series of experiments to explore new forms of in-service training. First it resolved that most short courses besides subject-updating should be school-focused, deriving from schools' assessments of their own needs. Second, that much in-service work should avoid the course format altogether – consultancy, inter-visiting and school-based development groups should be used. Third, that much of the leadership, consulting and tutoring should come from teachers themselves, who might need preparation for this distinctive in-service role. Both CET's early work on learning resources and the School of Education's first major in-service initiative, supporting schools preparing for the raising of the school leaving age, were handled in this kind of way.

Besides acting as a vehicle for the University's own contribution to short courses, the School of Education advises DES on their regional short course programme, and administers those courses that receive approval. In accordance with the above principles, the School has evolved procedures whereby its regional in-service committee sets up small development groups of teachers, advisers and lecturers to design and run courses in each specialist area, reserving to itself and DES the determination of overall priorities. Thus DES regional courses are jointly planned and jointly taught. The whole approach is nicely illustrated by considering the evolution of the current pattern of provision in school management.

The headteacher's role is fairly isolated, and advice and support not easily available. So in 1979 Tony Bailey convened a group of local secondary school heads to provide peer-group support for each other by meeting regularly, sharing experience and talking things through. After some time, a need for some joint activity was recognised, and they offered to run a DES regional course for heads of department. While that was being successfuly established, another head was able to set up an experimental course for heads who wanted to explore what industrial and commercial managers could offer them. Then in 1983 a Sussex Regional Management Committee, comprising headteachers, LEAs and industrial representatives, was set up to coordinate and develop management courses on a larger scale. When DES introduced a system of one-term training opportunities for experienced heads to be trained as management tutors and 20-day courses for these tutors to run for their colleagues, Sussex was able to build on this experience. Thus, in cooperation with six local authorities in the South-East, management courses have been developed that now have a national reputation.

This DES management training initiative heralded the beginning of radical changes in the way in-service education is to be organised and financed. Courses are to be self-financing and providers to charge appropriate fees. These fees, together with costs of providing supply teaching, are to be incorporated into LEA in-service programmes which DES both approves and funds. The University has focused its efforts on four main areas: management, science and computing, evaluation and pre-vocational education. A fifth programme aimed at the self-development needs of officers and advisers is now in a formative stage.

THE IMPACT OF CUTS AND PROSPECTS FOR THE FUTURE

If implemented, this new in-service system will suit the Education Area well, because it has been unable to protect the idea of dedicated posts during a period of cut-backs and retrenchment. When the Area was formed it had eight dedicated posts, which were not linked to student numbers. Four of these were in the School of Education for validation and in-service training. Now, with only one left, the short course programme has had to become self-financing. The four CET posts were largely for work on the improvement of teaching within the University itself. These were made more flexible in 1976 so that it became possible for members of Subject Groups to get part-time appointments within the University-wide Teaching and Learning Support Programme. But in spite of many positive contributions in all sections of the University, this programme was whittled down to a third of a post when the big cuts came. It is the one sector in which the Area has failed to sustain its early promise. The loss of these posts, however, is yet another reminder of the impoverishing effect of treating universities as if their only role was the batch-processing of students.

The effect of the cuts on postgraduate training and research is even more serious. The pressures of teaching more students with fewer staff are mounting. Post-experience students need and demand individual attention. Yet, when staff continue to provide it, they get less time for reading and research in schools. Hence less recent knowledge and experience is available for sharing with students. The circle is vicious indeed.

But let us end on a happier note. Once the major preoccupation with validation was over, the Education Area began to rethink its future. Its neighbour, the Centre for Continuing Education (CCE), with whom it has friendly relations and many common interests, was successfully wooed and the wedding fixed for September 1986. CCE has a complementary network of regional links and a similar experience of successful expansion followed by retrenchment and changing financial arrangements. We are both used to working with adults, and we look forward in particular to combining our resources in developing new programmes in mid-career professional education, where several new initiatives are already being planned and negotiated.

13

Thinking about Thought: The Cognitive Sciences at Sussex

Alistair Chalmers

In recent years a new subject has arisen on the borders of psychology, philosophy, linguistics and computing science. It centres on the theory of intelligent information-processing systems, of which the human mind is the central paradigm. Cognitive Science, as it is now called, draws its inspiration both from the enterprise of artificial intelligence, which stands at the leading edge of computing science, and from the study of human perception and cognition. The University of Sussex is a centre of excellence in both these areas...

The source of the quotation will be identified later. For the moment it serves to introduce this essay about an area of studies which, although it could scarcely have been envisaged by the founding fathers, began to emerge at an early stage of the University's development.

Cognitive science, in the current sense, barely existed as a distinct activity at the date of the University's inception. The first steps had, however, been taken in the two preceding decades, and some of the new Sussex faculty had begun to contribute even before their arrival in Brighton. For instance, Margaret Boden, then a very young Lecturer and now internationally eminent as an interpreter of artificial intelligence and its philosophical, psychological and social implications, had already published on the subject and had begun a major book before taking up her appointment in 1965.

More important for the University's immediate academic development was the choice of Stuart Sutherland to fill the

Chair of Experimental Psychology. His work on certain capabilities of visual systems combined theory and experiment in the development of a model which assumed more complexity in behavioural mechanisms than most psychologists for some considerable time past had been willing to recognise. At Sussex he set out to promote new work in which the insights gained in attempting to programme computing machines to perform complex tasks might be brought to bear upon thinking about problems of human performance.

Before going further it is perhaps necessary to indicate what was at issue here. Briefly, in the years between the First World War and the early 1960s many psychologists, in their concern for objectivity in observation and testability of hypotheses, confined themselves to studies of overt behaviour, often very simple forms of behaviour; and in their theoretical formulations they avoided reference to any complex processes, especially mental ones. Thus, for instance, language was treated as 'learned verbal behaviour' and was assumed to be amenable to explanation on the basis of what was becoming known about the conditioning of behaviour in animals such as rats and pigeons.

It is true that this kind of behaviourism was much less strongly espoused in Britain than in North America. This was due as much to the predominance of applied practice and the lack of interest in fundamental theory as to any preference for an alternative framework. To the extent, however, that there was an identifiably British contribution to psychological theory it drew heavily on engineering analogies, particularly on the principles of control mechanisms and, as they emerged, of digital computers.

In the mid-1960s Sutherland came close to obtaining substantial external funding for an institute combining behavioural, neurobiological and computational work on mechanisms of brain and behaviour. As has happened in the same field since (and will no doubt happen again) a fundamental researcher had come up with proposals which, at least in terms of funding, were ahead of their time. Despite generous pump-priming by the University, in the form of a UGC-funded building boldly authorised by the founding Vice-Chancellor, and the strong possibility that Sussex would attract, and therefore hold within the UK, a large share of the few outstanding talents available at that early stage, the Brain Institute (a title which still appears in working drawings of the University site) was not to be – at least not in its original form.

That episode, almost 20 years ago, was the last occasion on which the University stood ready to put substantial new funds into this field. The financial history since then has been a hand-to-mouth one of constituent elements of the University making redistributions within their limited existing budgets. This example highlights in retrospect the brevity of what at the time had seemed a prospect of much more extensive academic innovation.

Fortunately, although the Brain Institute as such did not emerge, Sutherland was successful in obtaining external support for many individual projects; and he pursued an appointments policy which brought distinguished workers in cognitive science to Sussex, many of whom were to have a considerable influence on the development of the field within the University and beyond. For instance, at the very beginning A. M. Uttley, following a distinguished career at the Royal Radar Research Establishment and the National Physical Laboratory, took up a research Chair to work on models of brain functioning and learning. It can be seen, then, that from the establishment of Experimental Psychology in 1965 the Laboratory was the locus of notable research activity in this field.

The first occasion on which the University claimed to be teaching something called cognitive psychology seems, as it happens, to have been in the Arts and Social Studies Area. The initiative owed much to the warm eclecticism of Marie Jahoda, foundation Professor of Social Psychology. Her conception of her field treated it not as a set of specialisms within psychology but as a perspective on the whole of the subject. This led her not only to a generous view of what sorts of person might hold appointments in Social Psychology but also to the recruiting of Margaret Boden, already in post as a Lecturer in Philosophy, to help plan and teach a new Major. Thus it was that the 1967–68 edition of the BA syllabus advertised *Cognitive Processes*, an introduction to human reasoning, problem-solving and computer simulations of these.

There were also other related interests in Arts and Social Studies, and it was not long before the time seemed ripe for a proposal that the School of Social Sciences should promote computing studies in some form. In its earliest version this was a suggestion for one element in a general expansion of the School. It soon became, however, part of the campus-wide planning for the 1972–77 quinquennium, the University's last expansionist discussion to date.

Preparation for 1972–77 was an elaborate business which began in the academic year 1969–70. All units, no matter how small, were required to produce unit plans. These were then debated and collated into successively higher-level documents, until the apex of University decision-making was reached. Some of the more dramatic elements were the proposals for various new Schools of Studies. The exercise certainly marked a decisive point in the development of cognitive studies at Sussex.

At an early stage Sutherland produced a comprehensive plan for a School of Cognitive Studies which would include Artificial Intelligence and Computer Science, Psychology, Linguistics, Logic and possibly, on an experimental basis, English Language and Literature. The intellectual focus was to be on 'the problem of knowledge and understanding', and it was noted that despite valuable intellectual connections the gathering of this array of disciplines under a single roof had not yet been achieved in any other UK university. Artificial Intelligence, the key discipline in these developments, had its origins in attempts to write computer programs which could be explored as models of human behaviour. This led to the development of extremely powerful software and programming techniques and, although the original aims remain, workers in the field also apply these tools to the creation of more intelligent machines. Whichever the emphasis, the research typically applies ideas about machines to humans and ideas about humans to machines, hence the close association with psychology.

The proposal was acknowledged to be timely in a number of respects, not least of which were the apparent drift of science sixth-formers away from traditional subjects and the increasing number of arts sixth-formers who were coming forward with some mathematics. The School might therefore prove attractive to students from widely differing backgrounds who wished to get to grips with new ways of thinking. Although emanating from the Science side of the University, the new School proposal had active support in Arts and Social Studies. Indeed, of the two completely new subjects to be introduced, one, Linguistics, was Arts-based; and most of the new School's proposed intra-University relationships were to be with Arts Area subjects. When the formal proposal was duly presented it was, although still very much in the form that Sutherland had given it, an Arts/Science document.

An important facet of the proposal was that the new School should be fully resourced at 'science' levels of space, technical support and funding. A working party chaired by the then Pro-Vice-Chancellor (Arts), Barry Supple, debated ways of making a start more cheaply. Sutherland, however, remained firm throughout on the need for a guarantee of ample resources from the outset, and the financial struggles of the Arts Area's own subsequent activities in this field suggest that his judgement of fifteen years ago was substantially correct. These resource implications proved the undoing of the project which, in the end, was not adopted as part of the quinquennial plan.

The internal discussion within the School of Social Sciences had meanwhile continued. Interests in promoting Computing and Linguistics there had coincided in a convenient way with the apparent need to initiate new patterns of study and find a new form of organisation to cope with continuing growth in student numbers. One solution was in the form of three separate, internally coherent 'Programmes', one of which was provisionally titled 'Communications Studies' and was projected to include both of the proposed new subjects. The term 'Artificial Intelligence' was not used in the documents, but descriptions of the courses in computing specified treatment of many features typical of AI programming (such as 'recursive procedures', 'list-like data structures' and 'the use of programming to study knowledge-based behaviour').

Although the proponents were also signatories to the Sutherland document there were important differences between the two schemes. Computing in the School of Social Sciences was to serve varied interests, including data analysis and formal modelling in Economics and other quantitative disciplines; and the overall aim was 'to provide an opportunity to study men *and social systems* in so far as they use linguistic and other symbolic structures either in individual thinking and reasoning *or in social interaction*' (emphases added). The University's quinquennial submission of September 1971 to the University Grants Committee identified, in addition to the more obvious disciplines, Sociology and Social Anthropology as subjects for which the new Programme was expected to provide a context. Also, the scheme envisaged a role for Linguistics that was not confined to its place in the new Programme, a hope that has happily been borne out. (It should be noted here that of the three possible Programmes discussed, Communication Studies was the only one which became a reality; and that as it developed in practice it lacked some of the more social elements originally envisaged.)

With the beginning of the new quinquennium the Programme was duly launched; and the trend of its future work was signalled by a change of title to 'Cognitive Studies' before the first student had been admitted. An immediately visible contribution from Experimental Psychology was the appointment of Max Clowes to the first post in Computing Studies. Clowes, an early English contributor to the development of Artificial Intelligence, had been attracted to return from Australia to an externally-funded research project in the laboratory. The post in the new Programme, although it had not been advertised as such, was upgraded to a Chair in recognition of his standing.

While others had been involved in initiating the enterprise, it fell largely to Clowes and Aaron Sloman to make it a full-blooded reality, and a more creative and energetic combination it would have been hard to imagine. It is scarcely possible to convey an adequate impression of Clowes' role to those who did not experience at first hand his enormous enthusiasm for his subject and his vivid personal presence. His decision in 1980, in spite of the pleas of colleagues and friends, to give up his Chair in order to concentrate on presenting significant developments in Artificial Intelligence to a wider audience was a great loss to the University, the sense of which was deepened by his sudden death only a few months later.

Sloman, a philosopher and ex-physicist whose enthusiasm had been fired by Clowes' vision of the potential scope of AI, was enabled by the award of an SRC Fellowship to go to Edinburgh to learn as much about the subject as possible in the space of twelve months. He returned not only having learned but, according to our colleagues there, having already begun to make significant contributions of his own. The assistance in obtaining funds for this Fellowship and the hospitality shown to Sloman are only part of the debt which Sussex owes to that other centre of cognitive science: a not inconsiderable number of our faculty have spent some significant part of their career at Edinburgh, usually at the doctoral or post-doctoral stage. The traffic, which still continues, is now bi-directional, but in the earliest years Sussex was very much the beneficiary.

Although Sloman was fully part of the new AI team from the moment he returned to Sussex, the small student numbers in the Programme restricted scope for teaching and it was fortunate therefore that his qualities as a philosopher were still much in demand. In general, the facility which the Sussex structure offers for introducing new activities gradually, and through collaboration across what would elsewhere be departmental boundaries, was absolutely essential to the development of Cognitive Studies in general and of AI in particular.

For ten years, in fact, most appointments in the Programme were sustained by the ability of the University to deploy faculty in varied teaching roles. The new Professor of AI, for instance, functioned also within the Social Psychology Group, and not in just a nominal sense: he carried the responsibility for one of the main compulsory courses in the undergraduate Major and was a powerful presence within the Subject Group throughout his tenure. Such meagre equipment and technical assistance as the Programme initially had, too, was transferred from other laboratories. The intellectual connections among the various disciplines are of course more important than these administrative ones. In a volume such as the present one, however, it is not inappropriate to stress the way in which the Sussex academic pattern made this kind of innovation possible in unpropitious circumstances.

The Programme continued to benefit from the creation of further new posts, albeit slowly, by internal transfer of resources which would have been much more difficult had strict departmental boundaries applied. The second new post in AI was filled by Steve Hardy, now sadly lost to the United States. One of his signal contributions was to the initial development of a uniquely powerful and friendly software system for cognitive science teaching and research, on what now seems in retrospect a ludicrously small machine. This became part of POPLOG (see below) which not only provided the main vehicle for the work of the Programme but has gradually developed into a commercially valuable product, the first whose revenue potential has been such as to lead the University to launch a jointly financed company to engage in marketing and further research and development.

The only other addition to the AI establishment, prior to the creation in 1983 of the national New Blood and Information Technology Schemes, was made possible by the generosity of the School of Engineering and Applied Sciences. Despite the obvious claims of that School, its then Dean, Dick Grimsdale, and the Chairman of the Electronics and Computing Science Group, David Woollons, supported a proposal that monies granted to the University for a new post under a limited UGC scheme to increase the number of 'microprocessor specialists' should go to the Cognitive Studies Programme. This has to be recognised as a significant gesture from a well-established but hard-pressed unit.

The other completely new subject which had to be introduced in order to make the Cognitive Studies Programme possible was Linguistics. This was by no means the achievement solely of the proponents of the new Programme. There had been substantial support for such a development in various quarters of the University, notably in the Schools of African and Asian Studies, Biological Sciences and Social Sciences.

The significance of this subject for the new developments lay in the concept of generative grammars. The essence of this approach is the formulation, for a given language, of a set of rules which although rigorous and economical in form, is sufficiently rich and powerful in its implications to generate a potentially infinite number of sentences. The relevance to cognitive science is that it offers a model, of rule-governed creativity, which can be followed by other sciences dealing with human capacities and behaviour; it lends itself to formulation in computational terms and therefore to wide generalisability; and the study of language as such is of central importance to the cluster of disciplines which make up cognitive science, for instance in the development of computer programming languages and in the understanding of human behaviour, including non-linguistic behaviour.

Linguistics got off to a flying start with the appointment not only of John Lyons, acknowledged doyen of the subject in this country and then Professor of General Linguistics at the University of Edinburgh, but also of a small group of outstandingly capable younger people who have engaged in joint work not only in cognitive science but with several of the University's Schools and Subjects, for instance European Studies and Social Anthropology.

The Programme is now, in 1985, on a path of steep growth in student numbers, attracting large numbers of well-qualified candidates. An undergraduate Major in *Computing and Artificial Intelligence* and an MSc in *Knowledge-Based Systems* are well established (the latter with extensive support from the SERC) and a further new Major, *Psychology and Computer Models*, began in 1985/86. As recently as the early 1980s, however, the numbers of students and faculty in the Programme remained small and there seemed little prospect of early expansion. The logistics still depended heavily upon the recruitment of undergraduates in the Social and Developmental Psychology Majors and it seemed to some in other parts of the University that the new developments in Linguistics and Computing Studies could not justify themselves financially. Nor, for some time, had external funding been particularly easy to come by. The Social Science Research Council was sympathetic but poor. The Science Research Council, although also providing some support, had not formally changed its decision of the mid-1970s, based on a specially commissioned report by Sir James Lighthill the distinguished Cambridge mathematician, to minimise spending in this field on the grounds, broadly speaking, that its promise was much less than had once been hoped and the difficulties much greater.

It is true that unrealistic hopes had been held out in fields of application such as machine translation, and that the achievability in principle of the original expansive aims of artificial intelligence was not demonstrable. But the restrictive attitude adopted in the UK in the 1970s and early 1980s can now be seen as an example of the hazards involved in attempting to legislate for scientific research and manpower planning. It is justifiable to claim that the University of Sussex was one of the few institutions which helped to maintain the vitality of the subject in a very lean period. Most notably, when in 1981 the University was obliged to plan for a reduction of 20 per cent in academic faculty it was decided, in spite of the poor student number prospects, to maintain AI and Linguistics at their existing strength. Then, just after, national bodies and the government itself were swept by a succession of sudden anxieties about new technology: the need for some kind of computing in all schools; the threat of the Japanese fifth-generation initiative; and the international position of the British software industry. Money began to flow in. Substantial contracts under the consequent Alvey Programme were awarded. (In number of such contracts received, Sussex, despite its small size, stands fifth among all universities in the UK.) In addition, a disproportionately large share of New Blood and Informational Technology posts in this field have been allocated to the University (two in Experimental Psychology and six in Cognitive Studies, one of them in Philosophy and Cognitive Science).

By this stage the University's record of research in cognitive science was outstanding. Work in Experimental Psychology had continued to develop independently. The building set aside for a Brain Institute became home for the Centre for Research in Perception and Cognition (CRPC), a research arm of the Subject Group. This not only provided excellent facilities for existing members of staff but attracted additional distinguished scientists, singly and in groups: the most notable among many were perhaps Christopher Longuet-Higgins, who chose to hold his Royal Society Chair at Sussex, and the MRC Perceptual and Cognitive Performance Unit. The high quality of many of the appointees to Experimental Psychology over this period has inevitably been marked by their subsequent departures for distinguished positions elsewhere in this country and the United States (as, for example, in the case of Phil Johnson-Laird, whose work on reasoning and language use was particularly notable). Even so, the Laboratory can still boast one of the most productive concentrations of cognitive scientists in Europe, supported not only by the usual project funds from Research Councils but in a more general way by excellent computational and experimental facilities provided under a large SERC rolling grant.

There is assembled in the Laboratory, for instance, a unique range of expertise in the study of language and speech, from the physiological coding of speech sounds in the auditory nerve, by way of detailed studies of the perceptual cues used in human listening and models of speech analysis, to computational modelling of language use in specific situations. A feature common to these areas of work, and to others such as depth, three-dimensionality and motion in visual perception, and on the perception of music, is the combining of computational modelling with psychophysical and neurophysiological experiment.

In the Cognitive Studies Programme some of the work has continued the Clowes tradition of research on machine interpretation of line drawings, extending it to more complex problems and to practical applications. In a rather different field, an achievement which has won international acclaim has been the development of General Phrase Structure Grammar by Gerald Gazdar, who has recently succeeded Lyons in the Chair of Linguistics. This is not only a major contribution to Linguistics but has opened up new possibilities in the machine analysis of natural language.

Other examples of interdisciplinary work are in the field of knowledge representation, where the analysis of distinctions among different formal logics has led to the development of systems which can reason about physical processes and to new techniques for building representations of axioms. Psychologists in the Programme have collaborated on computational modelling of cognitive processes in children of various ages, in the evaluation of psychological factors in software design and on human–machine interfaces in the design of expert systems. The widest interdisciplinary scope has been seen in the influential books of Boden and Sloman on the interactions between Artificial Intelligence and Philosophy and Psychology. Boden, for instance, has persuasively argued the essentially humanising character of AI's detailed demonstration of the complexity of many capabilities which we usually take for granted.

One special outcome of the work of the Programme has been the development by members of the Computing Studies Subject Group of the POPLOG programming environment, which has pioneered new tools for software development. This was adopted as part of the software infrastructure of the Alvey Programme, and is now being sold to both academic and industrial users in a number of countries. Central to POPLOG has been the provision within it of a powerful new language, POP–11, which is combined with other languages (LISP and PROLOG) in a unique way. The system is unprecedented in having been designed to suit both absolute beginners and advanced researchers or systems programmers. (It is, of course, extensively utilised by all classes of user in the Programme.) It is not just a programming language, or collection of languages, but includes within itself powerful editing facilities, the run-time system, and various types of on-line documentation, from reference material, through 'Help' files to actual tutorial procedures. The principal contributors to this remarkable system have been Cunningham, Gibson, Hardy, Mellish and Sloman.

The Cognitive Studies approach to using the computer as a tutor is somewhat unconventional. The wide range of student aptitude (found to be not closely correlated with formal qualifications held!) requires a very flexible approach which is achieved by leaving the student in control, working through 'Teach' files, free to jump backwards or forwards, with the computer in the role of advisor. POPLOG is, inevitably, heavy in machine usage, but this not yet fashionable approach is considered advantageous, given the present upward spiral in software development costs within a context of low hardware prices.

Presented with achievements of these kinds, and on a scale such that Cognitive Studies and Experimental Psychology each attracted £1,000,000 in research grants and contracts in the first half of this decade, it was perhaps not surprising that the University decided in 1984 to launch a new initiative in the field: the Institute of Cognitive and Information Sciences. Christopher Longuet-Higgins, agreed to become the first Director, and the words at the opening of this essay come from his statement of objectives. The Institute will be a coordinating body, encouraging collaboration among different groups within the University, providing a forum for researchers and graduate students, and promoting links with industry.

Its scope is to extend beyond that of the Cognitive Studies Programme and the Experimental Psychology Laboratory. It will build on collaborative links already existing with the School of Engineering and Applied Sciences, which enjoys a national reputation for work in fields such as computer image-generation, the architecture of computer networks and distributed systems, innovative graphics systems, application of knowledge-based systems to medical diagnosis and various aspects of control engineering and computer aided design and manufacture.

In addition, this collaboration together with the University's commitment to the new Institute has attracted industrial funds, from Eurotherm International, for a Chair of Computing Science which will be used to promote mainstream theoretical work in the middle ground between engineering and cognitive science. The Chair is to be located in the School of Mathematical and Physical Sciences, where the first occupant, Matthew Hennessy, will lead an additional, complementary stream of activity drawing in not only mathematicians but also some of the logicians in the School.

It has to be said, in spite of the euphoric tone of this report, that the story is one on which Sussex cannot be entirely self-congratulatory. There has to date been some lack of balance in academic computing activities; the University has still not been able to bring the allocation of internal resources to this field up to nationally prevailing norms; and the obverse of the flexibility which has made everything possible is a decision-making structure which has imposed its own far from negligible incidental costs. Everything has been hard work – very hard work indeed for some people. On the other hand, the efforts have been rewarded by the unstinting support of academic officers at various stages, from John Maynard Smith and Donald Winch, Deans of Biological and of Social Sciences in the early planning days, to the present Pro-Vice-Chancellors (Arts) and (Science), Margaret McGowan and John Murrell.

Certainly, the value of the interaction between teaching and research and the fruitfulness of the interdisciplinary environment have been amply demonstrated in this particular case. So too has the impossibility of legislating for research development. As recently as five years ago support for cognitive science was severely limited both inside the University and outside. Today it is not only widely acknowledged to be an exciting area of research in its own right but has become a factor of national economic importance. This is something that should be pondered by those who believe that research strategies can and should be determined by well-ordered bureaucratic processes.

It does not necessarily follow that cognitive science will retain indefinitely the status which it has recently attained. The history of thinking about cognitive processes is littered with discarded models which were based on the technology of their day but soon proved unequal to the task. The hydrodynamics of the seventeenth century and the telephone systems of the early twentieth are just two examples. Are the concepts of artificial intelligence going to be recognised in retrospect as nothing more than the fluid flows and switchboards *de nos jours*? Possibly, but not for some time yet. The digital computer may not be a tenable model of the brain, but the exercise of devising programs to emulate some of the capacities of human beings is distinctly productive, sometimes because it succeeds and often because of what is learned when it does not. What is more, the field at present attracts students and research workers of very high calibre. Those of us in neighbouring disciplines can look forward to the stimulating quality of an activity which, whatever its ultimate limits, is raising new questions and reformulating old ones.

Happiest of all are the evident drive and capabilities of a second generation of Sussex faculty. The present Chairmen of the Computing Studies Subject Group and of the Cognitive Studies Programme, Ben du Boulay and Mike Scaife, are both innovative young Lecturers; and in Experimental Psychology, Chris Darwin has just been promoted to a professorship. The incoming appointees to the Chairs of Computing Science and Computational Linguistics will be the two youngest professors in the University. The future seems assured.

14
Policy Research for Science and Technology

Christopher Freeman

THE ESTABLISHMENT OF THE UNIT

From the earliest days, even before the first buildings were designed and constructed, the University was envisaged as one which would provide a home for a variety of Research Institutes, Units and Centres alongside and within the various Schools. The first Vice-Chancellor, John Fulton, and even more the Pro-Vice-Chancellor in charge of planning, Asa Briggs, attached great importance to the encouragement of this aspect of University life.

Even though some of the many research organisations which were set up in those heady days of the 1960s have fallen by the wayside, the University has in my view benefited enormously from this strong and abiding commitment to research and to institutional innovation to facilitate it. The University has consistently performed well in the league tables of research funding, both in comparison with the other new universities, and in comparison with much older institutions. The capacity of the University to continue to attract support from the Research Councils, from foundations and from other extramural sponsors, even in times of great financial stringency, is a clear indication that this long-term strategy has yielded long-term benefits in terms of an enduring reputation for the quality of its research.

In any university, of course, a great deal of research can be and is undertaken on a part-time basis by the teaching faculty as a regular part of their normal activities. This research is complemented and facilitated, both by the work of post-graduate students and by the appointment of temporary Research Fellows and assistants and by an infrastructure of laboratory equipment and technical staff in the case of the natural sciences and engineering.

However, in some cases this normal mode of organising and financing research, both in the natural and social sciences, has not proved adequate to the needs of newly-emerging research areas, or the peculiar organisational problems in some fields of research, or the need to establish a critical mass over a sustained period. It was for a combination of these reasons that the founding fathers of the University were ready to commit themselves to a series of institutional innovations in order to attract and establish a variety of research activities, which gave Sussex a pluralistic pattern of research organisations, going well beyond the normal range.

One of the many initiatives of the early 1960s was in the field of science policy studies. The credit for this initiative must go to Stephen Toulmin, formerly Professor of Philosophy at the University of Leeds, and at that time leading a Nuffield Foundation project on the History of Ideas. As a result of his work in the history and philosophy of science and of his discussions with Asa Briggs, he became convinced of the need for an academic base for studies of science policy problems. Between 1961 and 1964 he discussed the idea with a number of universities, including Cambridge, Edinburgh and Manchester, as well as Sussex, and with the Department of Scientific and Industrial Research (this was before the days of the Science Research Council or the Social Science Research Council). He also had discussions with the first Minister for Science, Lord Hailsham.

There was a general although not unanimous view that his initiative merited support from government, industry and universities. But there were reservations as to whether a university mode of finance and organisation could cope with the problems raised by policy research in such a difficult and sensitive area.

This rather vague general feeling was not translated into any firm commitment to fund research activity on anything like the scale which Toulmin believed to be necessary. His discussions with foundations, with the DSIR and with colleagues at various universities did in the end lead to the establishment of new research and teaching at Edinburgh and

Manchester, as well as at Sussex during the 1960s, but things moved much more slowly and on a level which was well below his hopes and his convictions of what was needed. Sussex hosted a preliminary conference in 1963 and was willing to commit two posts from the then new Arts–Science Scheme to the establishment of a research unit of the kind which he envisaged. In the end, Toulmin decided that this was an inadequate basis on which to embark on a new venture of this kind and accepted the offer of a post in Brandeis University in the United States in 1964.

This was not the end of the story, however, and a few months later I was invited to launch the Unit albeit on a smaller scale. I accepted this invitation after it was agreed that in addition to the two Senior Research Fellowship posts, which the University was ready to commit, there should be an additional commitment to the appointment of a full-time Administrative Secretary and that this should be offered to Jackie Fuller, who was at that time working with me as a research assistant in the NIESR (National Institute for Economic and Social Research).

Although I thought it would be possible to attract extra-mural research support to the proposed new Unit, I was convinced that it would be impossible to sustain the operation without a minimal managerial structure, and that Jackie Fuller would be the ideal person to provide this. As it turned out, this was one of the best decisions I ever made, as the University accepted this condition, and Jackie Fuller's contribution to the Unit has been absolutely crucial ever since.

The second and equally important decision made shortly afterwards by the University was to offer the second Senior Research Fellowship to Geoff Oldham, who was at that time spending a year at OECD working on problems of science, technology and development. He had an unusual background, which included experience as a geophysicist with research and exploration activities in the oil industry in North and South America, and five years' experience as a Fellow of the Institute of Current World Affairs studying science and technology policy in China, Hong Kong and other Asian countries.

This experience proved invaluable in building up one of the

first major research programmes at the Unit – the Ford Foundation programme on Science Policy in Developing Countries – and a continuing stream of research in this field. It also led to an enduring emphasis on the international aspects of our work, which has certainly been one of the main strengths of the Unit ever since.

The University's decision to appoint Geoff Oldham and myself also embodied another fundamental principle, which has been a central feature of the Unit's mode of work – the joint activity of natural and social scientists. We have always been agreed that policy research for science and technology necessarily required such cooperation on a continuing basis. The University has consistently shown an understanding of the difficulties involved in developing this style of work by its administrative decisions, permitting us considerable autonomy, outside either the Arts or Science areas, while retaining close links with both.

In the early days of the Unit it resembled fairly closely the innovative small firm, often described and discussed in studies of science-based industries. Internal communications were by word of mouth, there was minimal paper-work, and decisions were made in an extremely informal and flexible way in response to initiatives from within and outside the Unit. Growth was fairly rapid, but it was organic growth, building on the strengths of those who joined the Unit in the first few years.

During the rapid growth phase of the Unit and the University it was possible to take decisions with a minimum of formality and time spent. When I used to meet Asa Briggs to discuss our activities in SPRU and ask his blessing for various new ventures, a typical meeting would last ten minutes and yield ten decisions. It was a good time while it lasted. More formal and democratic procedures inevitably evolved as we grew bigger and the University's management problems grew more complex. But we were fortunate indeed to have as a chairman of our governing body someone who knew our problems well, gave us enormous encouragement, and was able to give extraordinarily quick advice and decisions.

The present scale of the Unit's activities are nearly an order of magnitude greater than they were in the 1960s and there is no way in which the management of the Unit could have continued in the style of those days. But there have been at least two major elements of continuity. The first is that we have continued to minimise bureaucracy and time spent in committees, even though there is a high degree of participation in all major decisions. The second is that Denys Wilkinson, who succeeded Asa Briggs as Vice-Chancellor and Chairman of SPRU's governing body, has been equally supportive of what the Unit is trying to achieve in the more difficult circumstances of the 1980s. This continuity of support from the University has been a fundamental condition for its survival and growth. The present range and scale of the Unit's activities are now certainly far greater than any of us imagined in the 1960s.

Up and into most of the 1970s the Unit had two and a half tenured academic posts. But, as a result of a series of decisions in the early 1980s on the initiative of Geoff Oldham and the Vice-Chancellor, the University and the Research Councils agreed jointly to provide an increase in the core funding and UGC posts for the Unit. This has given it far greater strength and resources to achieve long-term objectives in research as well as enabling it to contribute much more to teaching in the University. By the end of 1984/85 the two and a half posts had grown to seven and a half tenured posts. In addition, in October 1984, the Economic and Social Research Council established a Designated Research Centre on Science, Technology and Energy Policy in British Economic Development within SPRU.

The Unit's budget during 1983/84 was £1.15 million. Approximately 13 per cent of this came from the University, 30 per cent from British Research Councils, 24 per cent from foundations, 15 per cent from government departments and government-funded agencies, 12 per cent from international organisations, and 6 per cent from industry.

The plan for 1985/86 to 1989/90 was drawn up in 1984/85 and provided the basis for the ESRC decision to establish a Designated Research Centre within SPRU.

The principal objectives of the plan were for the Unit's research to contribute to three major and related themes of enquiry:

1 Understanding, on a global basis, the nature, determinants and means of measurement of scientific discovery, technological development, and adoption and diffusion of innovations.
2 Understanding the problems of efficient management and evaluation of research, development and innovative activities at the level of the research organisation, the firm and national governments. This theme also includes studies of the effectiveness of policies designed to promote scientific and technological activities in industry, energy and services.
3 Understanding the economic, environmental and social consequences of technical change and their implications for policy.

These headings of the Unit's main research activities, as they appeared in mid-1985, cannot hope to convey either the detailed content of any individual project or the complexity of the relationships with sponsors in industry and government at home and abroad. But they do serve to convey the strength and breadth of the interest in the effects of technical change throughout the economy and in society more generally.

In fact, despite the increase in the scale and scope of the Unit's activities over the past 20 years, one of the main problems confronting the Unit today is how to cope with the constraints of physical space and managerial and administrative capacity to meet an increasing demand for science and technology policy research.

This raises two fundamental questions. First, is it right that this type of research should be conducted in a university framework, or would it be more properly or more effectively conducted within government, or in independent organisations? Secondly, do the achievements of SPRU itself justify the view that policy research is a legitimate and proper role for universities? The next sections of this essay attempt to answer these questions.

POLICY RESEARCH AND THE UNIVERSITIES

This section draws heavily on a review of the Unit's experience which I drafted in 1976 assessing the Unit's first ten years of activity. On re-reading it I was struck by the fact that the basic problems of conducting policy research in a university environment are still the same and that our experience from 1976 to 1986 has reinforced these conclusions.

The complexity of decision-making in government and industrial organisations has led to an increasing requirement for policy-related research. Since the 1930s many research institutes and groups have been established whose main concern is with policy problems. In Britain some of these have been at universities, but quite a number have been established as independent institutes (for example, the National Institute of Economic and Social Research, or the Policy Studies Institute). Still others have been established within the framework of government.

The experience of SPRU suggests that indeed there are some advantages in locating policy research at universities. Particularly important are the possibilities for postgraduate research and for teaching courses related to policy research. Other advantages are or should be the wide range of disciplines within the universities, high academic standards and an atmosphere of critical independence. To some extent the traditional forms of university research can exploit these advantages without the need to form specific research institutes or units. However, the fact that much policy research has been initiated outside the universities suggests that there are also difficulties in developing university-based policy research whether in specialised units or not. These should be frankly faced. The experience of SPRU as well as other university research suggests that they are not insuperable, but they can be severe.

On the part of some sponsoring organisations there is often a desire to keep policy-related research under fairly close control. This applies particularly of course to military, strategic and other types of classified research. But even in other policy areas, where no genuine security considerations apply, there is often a tendency to conduct research as an in-house operation, with restrictions on publication of results, and restricted contact with the academic community.

Even if a case for in-house research is accepted, this does not dispose of the case for complementary policy-related research conducted independently, outside immediate government control. Indeed, even in sensitive areas, such as foreign policy and defence, policy-makers have often come to the conclusion that there are benefits to be derived from independent research on the fundamental problems related to policy-making. Government departments, even those with their own internal research facilities, often also sponsor extramural research both on a long- and short-term basis. In the United Kingdom the Rothschild Report on government R & D specifically encouraged government departments to sponsor such extramural research both in the natural and social sciences. The Research Councils too have recently emphasised the importance they attach to policy-related research.

There are, however, also difficulties on the part of the universities. These are partly intellectual and ethical, partly organisational and financial. On the intellectual side there is a fear of becoming involved predominantly in rather short-term, narrow problems. On the ethical side, there are fears of subordination of the university traditions of free and unfettered inquiry to considerations of short-term expediency of particular governments or agencies of government. Organisationally, there are problems of sustained commitment to policy research and of the critical mass necessary to conduct effective research. Within the universities there are some who would argue that specific research institutes or units are not really necessary to achieve this. But there are problems of continuity of research and of overhead costs, which are not easily handled within the traditional framework of UGC-funded teaching posts and part-time research.

These problems are serious and there is a danger that, reinforced by the reluctance of governments to sponsor independent critical work, they may lead to the universities being by-passed or ignored as centres for policy-related research. This would have adverse consequences both for policy-making and for the universities. The dangers for policy-making are clear. There is scarcely any area of public policy where the basic understanding of the issues could not be substantially improved by research, and there are many where even an elementary theoretical understanding is almost completely lacking. In-house research is often and inevitably

constrained by time pressure and immediate policy considerations, and it must of course accept policy objectives. University research is somewhat freer of such constraints. It can
more easily extend its range to the examination of alternative
policy objectives. The intellectual resources of the universities
are certainly needed to complement other research activity.

Moreover, long experience has demonstrated the validity
of the traditional liberal position in relation to independent
evaluation of government policies. Many of the policy problems confronting modern government raise issues of such
complexity that the traditional roles of parliamentary opposition and the press, although essential, are no longer adequate. Consider, for example, the sort of issues raised in the
debate on choice of nuclear reactors or indeed the whole
post-war history of policy in relation to nuclear energy and
nuclear weapons. Margaret Gowing's scholarly history has
shown how weak and ill-informed were the public debates in
relation to issues of the greatest importance for the future of
the country. If the commitment of the parliamentary demo-
cracies to the idea that public scrutiny and debate are essential ingredients of good policy-making is to be anything more
than lip-service, then thorough independent research on
many aspects of public policy is a *sine qua non*.

Consequently, the difficulties in the relationship between
government (or industry) and the universities in the field of
policy research should be faced squarely. They can be sur-
mounted if there is understanding on each side of the requirements for policy research and the specific contributions
which the universities are best fitted to make. Clearly the
universities cannot be expected to abandon their commitment to open publication and debate. If governments have
genuine justification for restricting information and publication, then it is probably better not to involve the universities. For this reason among others SPRU has followed a policy
of refusing to take on classified research. However, our
experience suggests that there are not many areas of public
policy where this type of restriction can be justified and that
the traditional liberal view on open government is likely to
yield the best results in the long run. On several occasions the
Unit has had to insist on the principle of open publication in

the face of powerful pressures, including threats of legal action.

This does not mean of course that, within a general context of open discussion and publication, there may not be perfectly good specific reasons for some information being respected as confidential. This will normally be the case, for example, in relation to personal details of behaviour in psychological and social research, or some details of a company's financial situation and behaviour in economic research. There are well-understood and accepted conventions which govern the collection and use of such information, both in government and in university research, and the record of academic research is a good one in relation to the observance of these conventions. Nevertheless, those involved in policy research have a particularly strong obligation to observe them.

All of these considerations apply in full measure to research on policy for science and technology, and there are additional difficulties specific to this area of policy-making. One of these difficulties is that responsibility for policy-making is often widely diffused, and another is that policy-making does not respect the academic boundaries of the natural or the social sciences. It is these specific difficulties which have given rise to some of the peculiarities in the structure and mode of the work of SPRU.

Whereas in some countries a centralised responsibility for the main lines of policy for science and technology is clearly accepted and institutionalised, this has never been the case in the United Kingdom. Moreover, not only has there never been any clear-cut responsibility, but the pattern of pluralistic responsibilities has been subject to a bewildering succession of reorganisations and changes, even during the short life of the Unit. Councils, committees, advisers, coordinators and even ministries have come and gone. Periods of activist intervention in science and technology have alternated with periods of bland denial that there is any such thing as government policy for science and technology. The periods from 1970 to 1972 and from 1979 to 1982 were notable for this tendency. Other countries have experienced a similar flux in relation to the definition and location of responsibility for policy, although nowhere so extreme as in the UK.

The decentralisation of responsibility within the UK system, and the rapid changes within the organisations involved, meant that SPRU could not enjoy a special relationship with a single government department or sponsor, even if they (or we) had wished for such a relationship. Our sister research group at the University, the Institute of Development Studies, was established on this basis. But this option was never open to SPRU, since our pattern of work concerns many different agencies, with no single one predominating. This pluralism reflects the real situation in UK policy for science and technology as well as the strong international element in SPRU's work; it has, however, created a number of problems for the Unit.

The balance between longer-term, more fundamental research and shorter-term contract research and consultancy is one of the most difficult issues. From the outset the basic strategy has been to seek a combination of both types of work, on the assumption that policy research would benefit from direct contact with the live current problems posed by policy-makers in government and industry. Whether this is described as 'getting hands dirty' or 'feet wet', there is much to support the view that academic researchers who are not exposed to actual policy problems may suffer from sterility, remoteness from real life, and other vices and diseases of dwellers in ivory towers. There is also evidence that policy problems have stimulated advances in the social sciences (and, of course, that the development of technology has been a powerful stimulus to new advances in the natural sciences).

On the other hand, there is the real danger that a research group which conducts its research under contract for outside sponsors may in the end degenerate into little more than an instrument for objectives which are dictated primarily by considerations of short-term expediency. Under such conditions it is unlikely that any fundamental advances in knowledge could be made or published, and there would be little point in conducting such research in a university rather than in the sponsoring organisations themselves, or in a commercial contract research institute. These problems are most acute in policy research, since independent and critical assessment of the decisions of policy-makers may often be unwelcome to particular decision-makers and organisations. Yet from the long-term point of view and the wider interests of society it is just this independent, carefully researched critical analysis which is the most valuable contribution that a university can make to policy research and which alone can contribute to a deeper fundamental understanding of the issues.

To sum up this section: experience of SPRU suggests that despite the formidable difficulties of ensuring free publication and a balance of short-term and long-term work, the University of Sussex environment has proved a favourable one for science policy studies.

CONCLUSIONS

It is primarily for others to assess the achievements of the Unit and to decide whether these achievements merit continued support or not. So far as our own assessment is concerned, there are three criteria which we have applied in our own efforts to assess the performance of other research organisations, which might equally be applied to our own case. This concluding section does not constitute such a systematic assessment but is in the nature of a brief personal judgement using these criteria.

The first criterion is the crude and simple one of survival and growth. Since the Unit has passed this simple test over a period of 20 years, it does provide some indication that its work has been seen and valued as a response to some research needs of society. This is all the more true since throughout this period the Unit has been heavily dependent on extramural funding and this now amounts to over £1 million per annum.

In its SAPPHO project, which compared successful and unsuccessful attempts to innovate, the Unit established that responsiveness to the needs of users was one of the main features distinguishing success from failure. Obviously there is no simple analogy between policy research and industrial innovation. The users of our research results are a very heterogeneous group and the Unit sees its work more as influencing the climate and shape of policy debate and policy-making, rather than meeting the specific requirements of any individual client or user. Nevertheless, it seems that the Unit's work has passed the test of responding to a social need, both in the UK and internationally.

Over the same period quite a large number of attempts have been made to establish similar research groups in other universities in all parts of the world. We are delighted that some of these, particularly in Scandinavia for example, have flourished. But many have failed, particularly in American universities. There have been many causes of failure and it would take another SAPPHO-type project to identify them all, but among the most important were the following:

1 A failure to respond adequately to user needs, or indeed to identify users, in the sphere of policy-making.
2 A failure to contribute to the needs of the relevant university in the form of teaching and scholarly, published academic work.
3 The absence of an appropriate organisational and financial framework to satisfy these dual and sometimes conflicting requirements.

This leads on to the second criterion of research performance by which any research organisation, including SPRU, might be assessed. Obviously, simple survival and growth is an inadequate criterion in itself. It is essential to arrive at some assessment of the *quality* of research performance over an extended period. The traditional method of assessment is by peer judgement, but the Unit's own work on research evaluation, especially the work of Irvine and Martin, suggests that this can be reinforced by bibliometric and scientometric techniques. At least in the field of basic research, contributions to the published literature, especially in core journals and books, are an accepted mode of assessment of research contributions. Citation analysis has taken this approach a stage further.

Any such approach has to be handled with great care, because of the diversity of research fields, the importance of comparing like with like, the role of instrumentation, bias in publication systems, and so forth. In the Unit's case there is no doubt that it has contributed substantially to the international published literature in its own field of work over the past 20 years, and it is doubtful whether any other group in the world has surpassed it in the field of science and technology policy, or has been cited so frequently.

However, as we have seen, the Unit's work covers a diversity of topics and much of it overlaps with economic policy, energy policy, social policy, arms control and disarmament policies, development policies, and so forth. It is much more difficult to assess the Unit's contribution to these fields, although again I am sure that it has made a significant contribution to all of them as well as to basic disciplines, such as economics and sociology.

Finally, the Unit's work has to be assessed not only in terms of the response of users (conceived in the broadest sense), or in terms of contributions to published work and public knowledge, but also in terms of two other criteria: influence on policy-making and contribution to education.

Again, it is notoriously difficult to assess performance in either case. The Unit's contribution to undergraduate and postgraduate teaching was rather small in the first ten years of its existence, but it is now quite substantial, especially in the postgraduate area. The demand is there for still further expansion, especially in the post-experience field, but the organisational difficulties are formidable. The quality of postgraduate teaching and research has been uneven but some of the doctoral work has been first-rate, and has led immediately to publication. Paolo Tigre's thesis on the Brazilian computer industry won a national award as the best economics thesis in Brazil in 1984.

Influence on policy-making is the most difficult of all to assess. It would be possible of course for a research unit to do very good work in policy research, but for governments to disregard all their results. At the other extreme it would be possible to do poor research, which found early application in disastrous policies. All that can be done here is to indicate some areas where, in my view, good quality research has had a perceptible effect in changing government policies in the UK and elsewhere for the better.

One example is research on future demands for energy. The tendency in 1973, and for some years afterwards, in government and in industry was to extrapolate the high growth of energy consumption characteristic of the 1960s into the long-term future. This led to some very poor and expensive decisions. The Unit's work, especially by Surrey and Chesshire, showed that the underlying pattern of structural change and of technical change in the use of energy had led to a break in trend and urged a major downward revision of estimates of future demand. The Unit's team were in regular and close contact with those responsible for forecasting in the energy industries, as well as in the Department of Energy. Consequently, despite strong initial opposition, it was able ultimately to have some effect on energy forecasts and perhaps to help avert some even more wasteful and expensive investments.

Another example is the transfer of technology to Third World countries. A whole number of projects carried out by the Unit, especially by Oldham, Cooper and Bell in cooperation with researchers in Latin America, Asia and Africa, have demonstrated the limitations and dangers of the 'turn-key' packaged-plant approach to the import of technology and the extraordinary importance for the development process of building up indigenous technological competence and skills systematically, as a part of the process of importing and assimilating foreign technology. It is not too much to say that the dissemination of these research results and their theoretical generalisation has been a most important influence on technology policies in a whole number of developing countries.

A third and more difficult example relates to UK technology policies. The problem here has been to develop awareness in both industry and government of the crucial significance of technological competition in international trade performance, and productivity improvement. A whole series of studies in different industries and in the economy as a whole, notably those of Pavitt and Soete, have contributed significantly to a gradual change of climate, both among policy-makers and in the economics profession. This has had some perceptible effects in actual policy changes over the past ten years, but so far the policy response has in my view been wholly inadequate, for cultural and political reasons, rather than because of weaknesses in the Unit's analysis.

Finally, I take the example of arms limitation. Here the Unit's work has undoubtedly been among the best in the world on the relationship between new technologies and weapon systems. The work of Julian Robinson and Mary Kaldor has contributed greatly to the world-wide understanding of these problems and directly to the actual process of negotiating international agreements on arms limitation. It would be far too much to hope that any small research project could by itself reverse the escalation of the arms race or banish the threat of horrific weapons annihilating human civilisation. But if the Unit's work in this field could even to some very small degree help to banish this threat by contributing to effective international agreements limiting and preventing the diffusion of even more ghastly techniques, then this alone would in my view amply justify all of the Unit's efforts since its inception.

Afterword

John Fulton

This Afterword must surely begin with an expression of thanks to the University for inviting me to write it. Rip Van Winkle, as I remember, woke after 20 years of uninterrupted slumber to a succession of unpleasant surprises. I have been in retirement (though I hope not asleep) for almost 19 years: reading the second series of essays on the University of Sussex has for me been an almost unqualified pleasure.

The experience has forced me to think again, with whatever benefit hindsight can offer, first, about the beginnings of the University; secondly, about what on the evidence of these essays, it has achieved; and thirdly, about the problems that lie ahead.

I would like to have had space to dwell upon the qualities of the individuals who made up the original group on whom the responsibility of planning rested. Each was distinguished in his own field. They worked devotedly and harmoniously as a team. My recollection is that they were moved by a shared conviction that there were changes which they wished to see, changes that would be hard, even impossible, to bring about in existing institutions. So they willingly accepted the challenge for Sussex to innovate. I think that they would all wish me to mention exceptionally two names – those of the only two contributors to the first volume of essays (*The Idea of a New University*) who have not lived until the publication of the second: W. G. Stone, Director of Education for Brighton, whose persistence, in spite of repeated discouragements, in keeping alive the proposal for a university at Brighton, made possible all that was to follow – it was he who first proposed that there should be a place in the curriculum for European Studies; and Martin Wight, a devoted teacher and a profound

historian whose death before his time was a double blow to
Sussex and to scholarship. He had a quality, which he shared
with Patrick Corbett, that made me feel them to be, in a
special sense, the keepers of the University's conscience.

At the time when the University was opening its doors to the
first intake of students other events of great significance for
higher education were taking place. The Robbins Committee
began its work in 1961; and the Hale Committee on University Teaching Methods was working also from 1961 to 1964.
A pointer to general university opinion about the proposals
for new universities was the discussion devoted to this subject
at the Home Universities Conference in November 1960. I
was invited to lead the discussion with a paper on Sussex. I
spoke mainly of our intentions for Schools of Studies; for an
interdisciplinary curriculum in both Arts and Science; for
teaching methods designed to stimulate an active response
from the student; for projected speed of growth. The discussion showed that the interest of other universities was
focused largely on two issues. One was the dominance of the
single-subject honours degree, and its consequence in driving
the schools into premature specialisation. The other was the
balance between a university's twin responsibilities for teaching and research. It was more than once pronounced to be the
general rule that a preference for either must be paid for at the
expense of the other. It was further taken for granted that,
whatever protestations it might make to the contrary a new
university that gave its first collective thought solely to
education in pursuit of what Asa Briggs christened a 'new map
of learning' was in reality destined to be no more than a liberal
arts college – what Flexner (the author in 1929 of a much
discussed book on 'Universities – American, English and
German') dismissed as merely finishing schools. For him, the
quintessence of a university was research and the training of a
postgraduate élite.

Whatever the educational merits of liberal arts colleges (and
they are, on American experience, not to be lightly dismissed),
it never seemed to me likely, given the scholarly quality of the
group that did the early planning of the Sussex curriculum,
that the relegation of research and scholarship would be the
outcome of their labours. But, of course, experience would be

the test. So it was with no little eagerness to discover the answer that I turned to the essays included in this volume.

The first thing to notice is that there still remains an insistent imperative to 'get the curriculum right'. The social sciences established their case to form a School in their own right. The shape of Educational Studies had to evolve in response to internal and external pressures. An important battle had to be won against the danger of overcomplexity inherent in an interdisciplinary system of study: while innovation (e.g. Cognitive Studies) had to be absorbed and accommodated.

But in the presence of change and adaptation, the answer to the basic question – Are the major functions of teaching and research embattled against one another? – still comes out loud and clear. Not the verdict that early critics predicted; but rather that teaching in an interdisciplinary framework has stimulated and enriched the research of the teacher as well as the minds of the taught. New stimuli, new insights have arisen for both from the interplay of different disciplines. In the event, the University's achievements in research have been spectacularly good, as the Vice-Chancellor rightly claims: surely, unprecedently so for a university in the first quarter-century of its existence. If this continues to be so (and nothing within the University's own control seems likely to prevent it), the high hopes of our early days will have been truly vindicated.

I hope that before long the University will commission a history of the Institutes, Centres and Units – nearly a dozen of them – that have found their home on the campus at Falmer. A foretaste of the fascinating story they have to tell is to be found in the account given in the present volume by Christopher Freeman of the origins and growth of the Science Policy Research Unit. He makes clear that the interdisciplinary form of the University's academic programme was one of the chief, though by no means the only, magnets that brought it to Sussex and sustained its growth. Its wide and growing prestige has added to the University's high reputation for research.

The Institute of Development Studies came to Sussex after a long-drawn-out contest between different claimants. When I was Chairman of the Inter-University Council for Higher

Education Overseas, I was brought into close association with Sir Andrew Cohen, then Head of the Ministry of Overseas Development, the government department which established IDS. His qualities of heart and head and wide experience of government in London and Africa made him a redoubtable fighter for the cause of the Third World. He sympathised with the aims of Sussex, in particular its determination to establish an undergraduate School of African and Asian Studies. Without doubt he threw his weight into the balance in favour of Sussex. But he held firmly to the proviso that the Institute should be safeguarded against the dangers of academic insularity and introspection by an infusion on its governing body of international expertise and experience, together with repeated applications of what he described as 'mud on the boots'. He hoped, as I did, that its work would influence the teaching not only in the School of African and Asian Studies, but also in the social sciences as a whole. It would have pleased him had he lived to know how closely Anthony Low has linked, in his essay, the development of IDS with the story of the School of which he was the founder Dean.

Other similarly revealing stories would doubtless belong to others of the group – many of them since my time – who have joined their lot with Sussex. Their work has surely helped to lift its standing as a centre for research. Each has come to Falmer committed to a task which demands nothing less than academic discipline and expertise of the highest order. Beyond that their final goals lift the eyes of the University to large horizons: in the case of IDS, to trans-oceanic vistas and shifting balances world-wide between races and peoples preparing new destinies in the coming century; or, like the Unit of Nitrogen Fixation and the Centre for the Study of the Brain (as it was called in my day) to developments so vast and dazzling in their implications for the future of mankind that one could not resist their challenge to the imagination.

The verdict from the evidence of these essays is that the University is very much 'on its toes'. And that, despite hard times, the question that forced its way into all the early debates – What are we here for? – is still the touchstone of policy.

That question, however, demands an answer that is relevant to the times. And times have changed over the last two and a half decades. Among the changes we must include a different attitude over a large part of the developed world towards the costs and benefits of higher education. Robbins relied on the right of the individual qualified by ability and attainment to a university education. He did not, of course, deny that the society, which accepted the burden of the individual's education, was in need of his service. But he thought it impracticable to measure the extent of the state's financial responsibility by the yardstick of the future need for different kinds of skilled services. At best the answers could be used for only short-term projections: and higher education, like individual universities, by their nature can only be planned successfully over the long term.

To some considerable extent the balance of interest has swung away from Robbins. Hard-pressed governments increasingly prefer short-term, closed commitments to those that are open and last. So the universities have a case to make. More and more they are expected to justify themselves not only by their scholarly virtues, or by the demand for places in them, but by the social worth of their graduates.

We are concerned here not with the universities as a whole, but with one in particular. We have discovered from the essays in the present volume a great deal that was formerly mere speculation: the new curriculum ('getting it right'), remains a centre of intense interest – the theme recurs time after time. Research, too, flourishes in the studies and laboratories of Falmer.

But what of the Sussex graduates who have gone out to give service in the wider community? The University began its existence with a mandate 'to be different'. It accepted that mandate. It can hardly be the case that its graduates should be unaffected by the decision to adopt an interdisciplinary curriculum: teaching it has been pronounced a form of liberation; this in turn has enriched research. What has this meant to the students in the longer run? We have little to help us in answering that question from a reading of these pages. There are the interesting essays of the former students. But as the chapter head under which they write indicates, they are memories of undergraduate days rather than appraisals of what a university education did for them, or, in particular, what in the light of experience was special about being an undergraduate at Sussex.

Intermittently throughout the book we find revealing glimpses of possible answers. Donald Winch writes that Sussex graduates may have a special ability as communicators; Colin Eaborn writes of a new kind of 'Degree by Thesis' in his School and what it does for an enquiring mind: what makes those who chose that way different and what has happened to them since? Are they, in the modern jargon, specially good as 'problem-solvers'? John Maynard Smith lays it down that the education most relevant to his field must be in the principles that are most likely to be important in the whole lifetime of the undergraduate – something that was not provided elsewhere. In mid-life, are Sussex-educated biologists still noticeably better equipped with these principles?

From the start it was important that the Sussex student should possess the cardinal virtues of an academic apprenticeship. He must be taught (as Patrick Corbett wrote in his essay on 'Opening the Mind') to be active not passive; in other words he must leave the University knowing the 'feel' of thinking for oneself. Whatever his subject, he must have been led to seek to understand the patterns that govern the behaviour of people and things. In his own area of study the graduate should have learned to set aside his own prejudices and inherited attitudes, so that whether he operates in the boardroom or on the shop-floor; in the Cabinet or at the furthest outpost of government; in the headmaster's study or in the nursery school, he or she is disposed to seek the principles involved rather than resort to personal opinion. When personal responsibility is involved he must be able to 'take the discussion from there' with confidence, as well as to recognise the need when it is appropriate to refer to higher authority. He must be articulate in speech and writing; and successful in winning acceptance as well as encouraging initiative in others.

But then, may not these qualities be shared by universities everywhere? Perhaps they should: but we know that the graduates of British universities are different in important ways from those from universities in Germany, or France, and still more from those in the USA. We know that those from universities in Scotland are different from those educated at Oxbridge. Some claim to detect differences between the graduates of universities in the North and those in the South. It is far from pointless to seek an answer to the question, 'What makes a Sussex graduate different?' If the answer is that it is still too early to tell, could we put down a marker for the future? There is much at stake – the validity of the selection process; the system of examination; the choice of employment and subsequent careers. I hope that the University will now set in hand the task of finding the answers.

Index

213

Index

Briggs, Asa xiv, 1, 38, 54, 66, 97, 157–8, 159, 162–3, 166, 190–1, 193–4, 207
Brighton, relations with 17, Chapter 4 passim
Brighton College of Art 161
Brighton College of Education 4, 10, 159, 161, 166
Brighton Polytechnic 4, 10, 166–7
Brown, Michael 14
Bryant, Peter 132
Building Committee 5
Burke, Julian 133
Burrell, David 162

Caffyn, Sydney 7, 19
Carrington, Peter 106
Caston, Tony 154
Centre for Contemporary European Studies 12
Centre for Continuing Education 51, 54–6, 162, 164, 174
Centre for Educational Technology 11, 163, 164, 171–3
Centre for Multi-Racial Studies 13
Centre for Research in Perception and Cognition 184
Chalmers, Alistair 175
Charlesworth, Brian 132
Chatt, Joseph 115
Chelsea College of Physical Education 161, 167
Chemistry, see Molecular Sciences
Chesshire, John 204
Clowes, Max 130, 180–1
Cognitive Sciences 18, 90 chapter 13 passim funding 176, 183–4

graduate studies 183
Majors 183
Cohen, Andrew 12, 102–4, 106, 209
Colleges Advisory Board 165–6
Collett, Tom 132
Communication Studies 180
Community courses 55
Computing see Artificial Intelligence, Cognitive Sciences, Communication Studies
Contextual studies xii, 8, 72
Cooke, Jonathan 132
Cooper, Charles 204
Corbett, Patrick 158, 207, 211
Cornforth, John 114
Council (of the University) 16
courses
    common 70–1
    part-time 54
Cox, Denis 12
creative arts 56; see also Gardner Arts Centre
Crosland, Anthony 10
cross-subject teaching 7
Cultural and Community Studies, School of (CCS) xiin, 11, 67–8
Cunningham, Jon 186
cuts, government funding 7, 20, 23, chapter 2 passim

Daiches, David 66 and see Idea of a New University
Danielli, Jim 9
Darwin, Chris 189
Dean, Harry 41
Development Studies, M.Phil in 104
DES 10, 14, 161, 172–3
Dore, Ronald 103
Dow Corning Corporation 116
du Boulay, Ben 189

Index

Index

221